Normal Is Broken

By

Jeff Jones

Photography by God in Motion Ministries (GIMM)

2511 Publishing

8813 Beech Daly Road, Taylor, MI 48180

NORMAL IS BROKEN

TABLE OF CONTENTS

DEDICATION & CONFESSION

Dedicated to the memory of: Raymond & Geraldine Jones

Thank God for a heaven and roadmap to get there! So much to talk about, so much to be seen, but not so much for which forever cannot account. Looking forward to seeing you again!

I have failed at a long list of living at different times throughout my life. I have failed as a spouse. I have failed as a parent. I have failed as a pastor. I have failed as a son. I have failed as a brother. I have failed in my finances. I have failed friends. I may have failed you? I have failed in business. I have failed college courses. I have even failed before GOD too often.

One thing I haven't failed at though...and that is trying! As long as my list of failure, continue to grow, I am living. When this life in me finally fails, I lived trying to live. And this I do know, that my GOD will never fail me!

So in this oddity of words that have yet to fail, I find a failure proof truth. That failure is not defeat. That failure need not be forgotten; that in my failures others may find resolve. Failures; are a path way that define the victorious. And most certainly, that failing to try is the greatest failure of them all!

Better to allow a dream to break; then dare not to dream.

It is better to dare to fail; then dare not to try!

<u>Normal is broken: Prelude to Happiness</u>

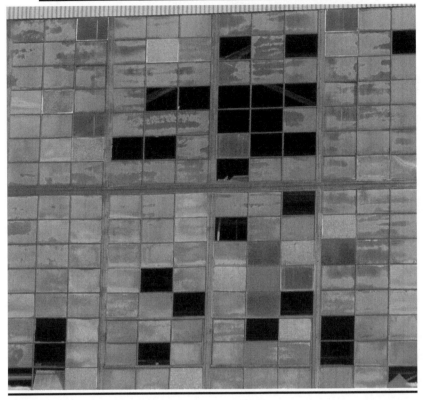

Procrastination has to be the greatest obstacle an individual faces. It seems to be the collection of all obstacles that appear at any starting gate. The start; is not that the actual obstacle to any venture? We then create the where, the why, and the how; mostly, around the reason and deductions that have influenced us. The people we have met, the scars of experience, the sour flavors of past failures, and the simplicity of human reasoning all grow like a volcano in the path of vision and success.

We tease about laziness, as we excuse our own lack of zeal to begin. We use "timing" as the other lie to deter us from our next greatest endeavor. Along with these, the ever famous funding lies. Do you really think with several national lotteries and specific local and state lotteries that generate revenues of nearly a billion a week; money is actually scarce on this planet? It is just not accounted for and you have to be creative enough to access its deep flow. This will all come to pass as you face the truth about the obstacles that you have lied to yourself about along with others that have lied directly to you.

Purposely, the word "procrastination" was used to start this iamb. It is the excuse and lie of procrastination that is the start of the greatest revealing you are about to experience about success, happiness, contentment, peace, and satisfaction. You see? It is that you just don't see!

We have been programmed to not see what we actually should see. We only look at this physical presence, rather than the truth that created it. It is in this truth that we live our lies. To live a lie is the most unsatisfying, unconscious, inexcusable, discontent of failures anyone could actually live. This breeds every rot of the mind, every reaction of disdain, and one of the greatest destructive truths that exists, "The <u>love of money</u> is the root of evil!". It is in the love of money that we lose sight of truth. It is because money is a façade, a lie, to hide the truth. Created by governments and man to manipulate ownership and continue with the most simple of magic; the great cup and ball trick. I will expose this and comment more elsewhere.

Here is the lie about procrastination. Procrastination is not your obstacle...Desire is your obstacle! It is in desire that worlds change. It is in desire that champions rule. It is in desire the underdogs overcome. It is in desire worlds are rounded, moons are landed, miracles come, and millionaires are made. Despite any single named obstacle, desire is all of ours! Is procrastination an object? No! It is a mental boundary!

It is a box created of untruths, doubt, fears, and the attack of the way we think. It is the truism of mind control. But desire, breaks us free!

Desire energizes. Desire gives new life, renewed vision, purpose, and the greatest of all...a passion for living! Passion is not just emotion. Compassion is emotion, but passion is life. It is alive. It beats. It flows. It moves. It responds. It creates and destroys. Desire is simply a change of heart. "As a man thinks in his heart, so is he." Would it be blasphemous to call this repentance? As my heart changes, my thinking and response change, in essence; when my heart changes my vision changes. What I see and what I don't see. I don't want to be distracted by the diversions and illusionists that live on the planet. What I want to see is my world. The lives that I value and the truth in which I choose to live. I may be your neighbor surrounded by similar circumstances, but it is my choice in the world I choose to live.

Physical law gets defied by creativity every day. It is in the planetary defines of skepticism, doubt, fear, negativity, and destructive words that degeneration exists. Scary thoughts like eternal life, optimism, renaissance, and rebirth are the promotions of dreamers. It is the dreamers that give us a world in which to live. It is their words, the results of their thoughts, resonance of their heart. It is their desires that overcame the lying obstacles of their lives. Tell that to Abraham, to Moses, to Solomon, to Christopher Columbus, and DaVinci. Tell it to Edison, Ford, Einstein, and Rockefeller. Tell it to Ziglar and get embarrassed. Tell it to your Creator and get laughed at in your calamities.

Desire to be! When you plant desire in your heart all things become possible. Desire truth and you will conquer your world. Desire destroys procrastination like a crystal ball dropped on concrete.

Desire sees what others do not see. It is in desire, not lust, wood kindles. When you come to see the truth that life is not chains or circumstance, but rather the creating of a vision for living that obstacles do not actually exist. This is not hype! This is orchestrated truth. Your eyes have been blinded, your minds darkened, and your vision subliminally disfigured. What if everyone could be happy? What if satisfaction was not the overthrow of others? What if there was a truth that violated time, physics, and dynamics? Would you want to know more about it? What if you could see what others do not see? Would that be enough? Read on then, you have been challenged to become unchallenged! Is not that what life really is, a series of opportunities to see what others do not see?

Go live life!

CHAPTER 1

How Do You Identify Your Obstacles

How do you define your obstacles...let alone identify them? Most of us have made our obstacle excuses. Excuses are not obstacles....just mental road blocks! It is in the mental road blocks of our lives that limitations occur. It is in limitations that dreams are shattered, joy dissolves, opportunity vanishes, and even worse, ideas get run off a cliff! Imagine; if you have any imagination left, what the world would be like without limitations? I am not talking about limitations of right and wrong, although most of that is without justification; I am talking about the limitations of: fear, faithlessness, laziness, procrastination, doubt, envy, and jealousy. These are the emotional, spiritual, and misguided limitations that manifest themselves into physical and psychological depravity. Yes, depravity that disables, discourages, and disavows living.

When we have finally identified our excuses into obstacles, we then can analyze that our obstacles are not what we see, but what we cannot see!?! It is in what we cannot see that we define the subliminal of our lives. The lies that others have incepted into us, let alone, out of which, the living we have excused ourselves. It is in these identifications that reality actually exists. We live within some sheltered fantasy of self-created nightmares and blame others of the reflections and shadows that possess us throughout the day. It is bad enough to let the images of the dark get exaggerated into the hideous. I have imagined into existence many a demon. Yet that is not too far from the truth at all!?!

The things that have strangled me, restrained me, fought with me, and exhausted me, are a very generous lengthy list. With a smirk and a jerk, they vanish? AMAZING!?! Is it not? Outrageous!?! Yes, it is! To find myself sleeping on my arm, a pillow between my legs, a dry throat, a bad meal, a few pharmaceuticals and you have yourself the perfect Stephen King novel. It is usually not that simplistic, but these are some potential ingredients?   This is not skepticism. Many demons go bump in the night.

Many dreams are in need of requiring interpretation. Many stories need to be told. Yes... and many creative minds get cluttered from expression.

It is a regular occurring event for me to get up in the middle of the night and turn on the light, step into the dark, walk towards the bump, or reason out from beneath the covers the amorphous shapes and whispering sounds of the 3am. The dangers of creativity are not too threatening...only to share them is the dare! The folly and ridicule that is brought by those in the "light" is absolutely disgraceful. Not the now of you, but the past of them. It is the moments of us that life is lived. It is in these moments that ideas surge, hearts beat, lungs breathe, thoughts pass, and passion rages, oh, impetuosity?

I purposely quoted "light", aforementioned. It is here, in the know, in the light, in the seeing that is where believing exists. This is where the blind live. This is where the disciple Thomas lived. Not in the truth of what was spoken or encouraged to pursue, but in the flesh, the touch of things, the seeing is where so many live. People say they are believers, but believers of what?

Believing of what they see; or what others have seen; or what others heard. Experiencing the things they have touched; and felt; and squeezed; and manipulated; and controlled; and limited; and cooked; and baked; and exploded; and destroyed.

This is the idiocy of religion; the creations of mankind. The defining of denominationalism are the perimeters of a prison for faith. The long list of ruler-ship, manipulation, and control creating an ache for the long trail of blood throughout generations that attempted to force truth to fit the boxes of inquisition. The genocide and grotesque tortures of those that didn't fit into the bag of tricks is a travesty. Oh the groaning of my soul to walk in the Spirit of Truth, and get outside of me to live.

Being raised in a home that was of traditional and social confines of influence, especially in the realm of religiosity, it had its limitations. Although learning compassion for mankind was a great plus; it was being taught within the eloquence of a captive and controlled audience, dare I say held hostage by tradition?

As my Pandora opened, I was launched into the powers of evangelistic truth. As into the Wonderland I fell, so did compassion, along the heart of realization.

The realization that people were people and this is not Beulah Land. That the Holy Spirit of God didn't need more salespeople, but more salespeople needed the Spirit of God! Knowing that truth was a treasure to share, not to force others to swallow, was an epiphany!

I am unmovable in my faith! I will take the challenge of the most skilled chess player on the matters of biblical truth, salvation, justification, and eternal redemption. My righteousness is not based on me, but on Him who stood my trial and took my punishment. He then offered me forgiveness. Double Jeopardy is a biblical truth! I will not stand trial for sin, because I trusted in the One who already did. I cannot be brought back into the court room and tried again, not only for the crimes that were already condemned, but the crimes that would ever be.

The greatest principle and truth in the whole of the universe is that Christ took my blame, suffered my punishment, or bought my redemption, and then forgave me for what caused His shame, persecution, and death. Because, in His resurrection he triumphed over the hell we all deserved.

I didn't have to see this event or experience it, in order to receive the truth of it. Lucifer could give a much more detailed event and description of what took place, right down to the looks on people's faces and where the drops of blood fell. Knowing the story is not the same as believing the story!?!

I cannot touch it, taste it, or see it...yet I believe it. In this undefined space, this so distant of time and reality, I receive the essence of eternity; unconfined, unbounded, free fall, into faith!

The most bewildering story is that for those that lived with Jesus, followed him, "loved" him, eaten with him, fished with him, heard the stories, the truth, and the experiences of the miraculous, couldn't believe what he had told them?

In chapter twenty of the book of John an amazing story is told.

The first day of the week cometh Mary Magdalene early, when it was yet dark, unto the sepulchre, and seeth the stone taken away from the sepulcher.[2] Then she runneth, and cometh to Simon Peter, and to the other disciple, whom Jesus loved, and saith unto them, They have taken away the LORD out of the sepulchre, and we know not where they have laid him.[3] Peter therefore went forth, and that other disciple, and came to the sepulchre.[4] So they ran both together: and the other disciple did outrun Peter, and came first to the sepulchre.[5] And he stooping down, and looking in, saw the linen clothes lying; yet went he not in.[6] Then cometh Simon Peter following him, and went into the sepulchre, and seeth the linen clothes lie,[7] And the napkin, that was about his head, not lying with the linen clothes, but wrapped together in a place by itself.[8] Then went in also that other disciple, which came first to the sepulchre, and he saw, and believed.⁹ For as yet they knew not the scripture, that he must rise again from the dead.¹⁰ Then the disciples went away again unto their own home.¹¹ But Mary stood without at the sepulchre weeping: and as she wept, she stooped down, and looked into the sepulchre,¹² And seeth two angels in white sitting, the one at the head, and the other at the feet, where the body of Jesus had lain.¹³ And they say unto her, Woman, why weepest thou? She saith unto them, Because they have taken away my LORD, and I know not where they have laid him¹⁴ And when she had thus said, she turned herself back, and saw Jesus standing, and knew not that it was Jesus.¹⁵ Jesus saith unto her, Woman, why weepest thou? whom seekest thou? She, supposing him to be the gardener, saith unto him, Sir, if thou have borne him hence, tell me where thou hast laid him, and I will take him away.¹⁶ Jesus saith unto her, Mary. She turned herself, and saith unto him, Rabboni; which is to say, Master.¹⁷ Jesus saith unto her, Touch me not; for I am not yet ascended to my Father: but go to my brethren, and say unto them, I ascend unto my Father, and your Father; and to my God, and your God.¹⁸ Mary Magdalene came and told the disciples that she had seen the LORD, and that he had spoken these things unto her.¹⁹ Then the same day at evening, being the first day of the week, when the doors were shut where the disciples were assembled for fear of the Jews, came Jesus and stood in the midst, and saith unto them, Peace be unto you.²⁰ And when he had so said, he shewed unto them his hands and his side. Then were the disciples glad, when they saw the LORD.²¹ Then said Jesus to them again, Peace be unto you: as my Father hath sent me, even so send I you.²² And when he had said this, he breathed on them, and saith unto them, Receive ye the Holy Ghost:²³ Whose soever sins ye remit, they are remitted unto them; and whose soever sins ye retain, they are retained.²⁴ But Thomas, one of the twelve, called Didymus, was not with them when Jesus came.²⁵ The other disciples therefore said unto him, We have seen the LORD. But he said unto them, Except I shall see in his hands the print of the nails, and put my finger into the print of the nails, and thrust my hand into his side, I will not believe.²⁶ And after eight days again his disciples were within, and Thomas with them: then came Jesus, the doors being shut, and stood in the midst, and said, Peace be unto you.²⁷ Then saith he to Thomas, Reach hither thy finger, and behold my hands; and reach hither thy hand, and thrust it into my side: and be not faithless, but believing.²⁸ And Thomas answered and said unto him, My LORD and my God. ²⁹ Jesus saith unto him, Thomas, because thou hast seen me, thou hast believed: blessed are they that have not seen, and yet have believed.[30] And many other signs truly did Jesus in the presence of his disciples, which are not written in this book:[31] But these are written, that ye might believe that Jesus is the Christ, the Son of God; and that believing ye might have life through his name.

So let me recap: Here is a team of discouraged, disappointed, disillusioned, and disparity is an understatement. Not because of truth, but because of what they saw. They placed no faith in truth. You see? Truth is not bound by time. It is not bound by our time, relative time, or even the vibration of a cesium atom? They, the team of world changers, the conduit to humanity, the students of the divine, had lost vision. But it was the vision they had perceived, rather than the truth of which they could not! The whole lot had lost sight of the things that had been taught. Not that they did not have the best of teachers, but they chose not to see what was actually before them. They had become students of parables, signs, and dependency. Much like the world we live in today.

An attorney once told me in response to my questioning; "Jeff, this is order in chaos". Things are made to appear as they are, because no one cares to see beyond what they perceive.

The power of this story, this magnifying truth, is that it is simply your choice. You can accept this, or you can reject this. This is not for me to measure you, only to open you up to even greater truth's to live and enjoy. To walk you into the eternals is an adventure so worth taking! It settles my destiny, my questioning, my doubts, my fears, and my directions. This makes life more simple, as well as, allowing me to see what others may not. This breeds peace, contentment, authority, and purpose. These are empowering tools for life. Like any tool, any language, any truth, if left unstudied, untrained, undisciplined, unexplored is futile. Think on it? Selah!

Who was this Thomas? What had he heard? What had he experienced in this life that made him so skeptical? Was it not what he had seen? Was it not what he had experienced? Was it not what was in his head and not his heart? Jesus did not appear because of his head thoughts or his own will power. The truth already existed. Thomas' skepticisms were brought on by what he could not see. Like many others, we live our lives based on our own experiences and visualizations that we have conceived. This is the manifestations of doubt. The continuance of box living. The very things that create mental obstacles as real as they may seem, we have proved them to be truth in our limited box of thought. The conviction of what makes sense to us.

So we live in the skepticisms that others are living a lie. Hope is not real. Dreams do not come true. I am alone in this world and the expression 'dog eat dog' is the real reality. My thoughts are; if the dog wants to eat it, he can have the trash. You are not the animal. You are not animalistic! You have hope. You have reason. You have choice. You have desire. You have dreams to accomplish. You have purpose. You have direction. You do not live in a cage, because you are not an animal. If anyone tries to cage you, it is a good idea to map your escape. That goes for governments, relationships, employment, and religion. If you cannot have questions that need to be answered without condescension or disdain, you have found yourself outside of capable leadership.

I have for years attempted to master the recital of Romans, chapter 8, in the New Testament.

There is, therefore now no condemnation to them which are in Christ Jesus, who walk not after the flesh, but after the Spirit.[2] For the law of the Spirit of life in Christ Jesus hath made me free from the law of sin and death.[3] For what the law could not do, in that it was weak through the flesh, God sending his own Son in the likeness of sinful flesh, and for sin, condemned sin in the flesh:[4] That the righteousness of the law might be fulfilled in us, who walk not after the flesh, but after the Spirit.[5] For they that are after the flesh do mind the things of the flesh; but they that are after the Spirit the things of the Spirit.[6] For to be carnally minded is death; but to be spiritually minded is life and peace.[7] Because the carnal mind is enmity against God: for it is not subject to the law of God, neither indeed can be.[8] So then they that are in the flesh cannot please God.[9] But ye are not in the flesh, but in the Spirit, if so be that the Spirit of God dwell in you. Now if any man have not the Spirit of Christ, he is none of his.[10] And if Christ be in you, the body is dead because of sin; but the Spirit is life because of righteousness.[11] But if the Spirit of him that raised up Jesus from the dead dwell in you, he that raised up Christ from the dead shall also quicken your mortal bodies by his Spirit that dwelleth in you.[12] Therefore, brethren, we are debtors, not to the flesh, to live after the flesh.[13] For if ye live after the flesh, ye shall die: but if ye through the Spirit do mortify the deeds of the body, ye shall live.[14] For as many as are led by the Spirit of God, they are the sons of God. For ye have not received the spirit of bondage again to fear; but ye have received the Spirit of adoption, whereby we cry, Abba, Father.[16] The Spirit itself beareth witness with our spirit, that we are the children of God:[17] And if children, then heirs; heirs of God, and joint-heirs with Christ; if so be that we suffer with him, that we may be also glorified together.[18] For I reckon that the sufferings of this present time are not worthy to be compared with the glory which shall be revealed in us.[19] For the earnest expectation of the creature waiteth for the manifestation of the sons of God.[20] For the creature was made subject to vanity, not willingly, but by reason of him who hath subjected the same in hope,[21] Because the creature itself also shall be delivered from the bondage of corruption into the glorious liberty of the children of God.[22] For we know that the whole creation groaneth and travaileth in pain together until now.[23] And not only they, but ourselves also, which have the firstfruits of the Spirit, even we ourselves groan within ourselves, waiting for the adoption, to wit, the redemption of our body.[24] For we are saved by hope: but hope that is seen is not hope: for what a man seeth, why doth he yet hope for?[25] But if we hope for that we see not, then do we with patience wait for it.[26] Likewise the Spirit also helpeth our infirmities: for we know not what we should pray for as we ought: but the Spirit itself maketh intercession for us with groanings which cannot be uttered.[27] And he that searcheth the hearts, knoweth what is the mind of the Spirit, because he maketh intercession for the saints according to the will of God.[28] And we know that all things work together for good to them that love God, to them who are the called according to his purpose.[29] For whom he did foreknow, he also did predestinate to be conformed to the image of his Son, that he might be the firstborn among many brethren.[30] Moreover whom he did predestinate, them he also called: and whom he called, them he also justified: and whom he justified, them he also glorified.[31] What shall we then say to these things? If God be for us, who can be against us?[32] He that spared not his own Son, but delivered him up for us all, how shall he not with him also freely give us all things?[33] Who shall lay anything to the charge of God's elect? It is God that justifieth.[34] Who is he that condemneth? It is Christ that died, yea rather, that is risen again, who is even at the right hand of God, who also maketh intercession for us.

35 Who shall separate us from the love of Christ? shall tribulation, or distress, or persecution, or famine, or nakedness, or peril, or sword?36 As it is written, For thy sake we are killed all the day long; we are accounted as sheep for the slaughter.37 Nay, in all these things we are more than conquerors through him that loved us.38 For I am persuaded, that neither death, nor life, nor angels, nor principalities, nor powers, nor things present, nor things to come,39 Nor height, nor depth, nor any other creature, shall be able to separate us from the love of God, which is in Christ Jesus our Lord.

It is in the spirit of truth that we change ourselves. It is in the spirit of truth that we grow. It is in the spirit of truth that we learn to walk away from the things that makes us feel what we define as real. This is the darkness of our lives. This is the temporal and the vain; the mutated and manipulated.

2 Corinthians 4:18 While we look not at the things which are seen, but at the things which are not seen: for the things which are seen are temporal; but the things which are not seen are eternal.

This is where spiritual wickedness reigns, and the flesh exhaust itself in shadow boxing.

Ephesians 6:12 For we wrestle not against flesh and blood, but against principalities, against powers, against the rulers of the darkness of this world, against spiritual wickedness in high places.

What you see is not your battle; it is what you don't see that is. Like the façade of love today... love is not what you get ... love is what you give. Peace is not what you get, peace is what you possess. Good will is not what you expect, but rather good will is what you live. We all have a perfect, acceptable, and good will with our Creator. Many never find the perfect relationship with the Glorious because they never employ the goodness at the start.

What is acceptability? Is it acceptable to reason out what others should do or be? Or is it more justifiable to determine what is not for you to do or to be? We rarely see ourselves. In fact, we never actually do; only a reflection, a reverse negative. WOW! What a truth is that?

What you may have reasoned down to rhetoric is just the beginning of the layers we have evolved around us. I may not accomplish all my dreams, stand atop all my mountains, or overcome all my obstacles. I may die looking up at what I have yet to complete, but I most certainly will not live my life looking up at others accomplishing their dreams, climbing their mountains, and overcoming their obstacles, with the downward look of excuses and defeat!

A rare old friend, Homer Batterson, once told me; "Jeff, you are bulldog tenacious!" "If you say we are going to take that hill, by Gosh, we are going to take that hill!"

Homer the Warrior, legally blind living amongst thousands of antiques and old newspapers, mailings, and roaming cats, never promoting his accomplishments with Dorsey, and other great musicians of the wartime bands. Homers dreams were shattered by his wife's death of many years. He just survived her. We had planned a lunch together. I went to pick him up as usual, but he was not there? He had leukemia that had been in remission for over ten years. But in a fragment of time, it turned acute. We went from conversation to good bye in a matter of hours. It was unbelievable?!? When I realized he wasn't home, I just assumed his age had got the best of him and he took up a better offer for the day? I drove home to receive a call that he had been hospitalized a few hours ago and it would be best I go see him.

It was a good Michigan winter with plenty of snow and cold and they took him to a hospital 50 miles away. I went straight to see him. He was slightly unconscious from sedation and the nurse said he was moments from leaving. I visited him with one sided conversation and was shocked that the hospital had him pegged for a new address so soon? Finally, I took his hand and kissed his forehead and said it was ok to go see his wife and his Savior. They would be waiting with joyful smiles and glad hearts. I went down several levels to the lobby, walked to my car, and the nurse called and said Homer just died. I quickly corrected her and said, "NO, mam you are mistaken" She interrupted abruptly and said no sir you are mistaken he has died I am very sorry to tell you this. I finished; "You see death, I see life!" "Homer passed from death unto life...and if this is death, I cannot wait for life! My view changed my perspective which changes my thinking which changes my world.

I live on your planet, but I may live in another world. Many use this expression as a criticism. "You live in another world!" I say ..."Thank God, I do!" You see? I live in the truth that I don't live to die, I die to live. Taking care of that decision, changes my whole reasoning for living. When I came to settle the end of my life, it made the rest of my life worth the living!!! I love the song, "live life like your dying"! I would like to have a second or two on a bull named Foo Man Chu. I want to find out what it is like to ride a drop of rain. Experience is the adventure of living though....not of dying. I am happy many have a bucket list. But, WOW what a trade to have a moment by moment life platter; a continuing collection of adventures, memories, and overcoming of obstacles.

After Homer had changed addresses, his estate was handled by some longtime friends. Many had seen Homer as a weak fragile old man. Humped over by cares and burdens and blinded by macular degeneration, Homer the Hermit had been hidden by weeds and decay. He lived easily and quietly in his abandoned little village. I have no idea how many thousands of dollars were generated at his auction? Old Conklin museum pieces, Base cellos, violins, piano turning kits, assorted musical instruments, and a wide range of antiquity sprawled the side yard. It was the old Duncan Fife dining table that started my bidding. I eventually was outbid and was leaving empty handed, when the auctioneer asked me if I still wanted the table set. I was elated! Someone who outbid me remembered my relationship with Homer and gave the table up for my last bid. It was old, but it looked as if it never had been used. For years it was buried under unopened mail, news, and magazines, as well as, custom made leather and felt pads to protect the finish. As I loaded it up in a van, the crew said, make sure you get all of the accessories. "What accessories?" They led me to a large crate and tarp. Nestled unused under cover were 6 more chairs and a box of leafs. It was a twelve seat dinner set with expanding folds! It was gorgeous as is, but with the hidden pieces it became a priceless treasure! It was the unseen that created the tremendous value.

Not only in my find, but to the whole community, as collectors far and wide that opened history long forgotten. Homer travelled with Dorsey in a wartime band! He was gifted not only as musician, but had built quite a reputation for piano tuning and teaching with his wife. He would tell me of these days over hot cocoa or tea. He would paint the most beautiful pictures of frivolity and lighter days of love and revelry. "Take the hill, Jones!" He would gravel! We would smirk and I would forge on.

CHAPTER 2

Fear Is Not your Obstacle

Fear is not an obstacle, Truth is! I love the quote of Will Smith in After Earth; "Danger is real, fear is a choice." The essential truth of this statement is that danger requires strategy. I believe in a well-defined plan. I appreciate documented schedules. I recognize that there are circumstances that initiate priority, but fear is the simplicity of experiences and choices of the undefined.

Fear is the absence of faith and faith is the understanding of truth. I am not talking hype. I believe I could hype myself across a bed a burning coals. I could hype myself into a good scrap, but it takes truth to get me through to victory.

When I was a teenager I enjoyed playing every sport. Not that I was a good at everything I did, but I enjoyed the competition, interaction, and personal challenges. I believe team sports are my favorite because of the beauty of synchronized truth. But in individual sports, it is the truth of preparation that defines the victory. I always believe "want to" can go farther than talent, yet it is in the knowledge and experience that separates the amateur from the professional. As I wrestled my first year in ninth grade, I was taken to a new level of personal training. To do a pull up was difficult at one hundred and sixty –five pounds. A chin up was nearly impossible! Two variables I had to work on, arm strength and lose weight!

I had played organized baseball for seven years. I had played organized football for four. But this sweating out pounds and taking my body beyond where it has ever been or anyone had gone before was totally Star Trek! I hurt in places I didn't know could hurt? I did push-ups, pull-ups, and chin ups until I strained my cartilage between my ribs and was rushed to the emergency for I didn't know what was happening?

All that to say; I got stronger, faster, and more skilled. I was the middle linebacker animal on the defensive team, But I was PUMA SUMA on the mat. I couldn't wait for someone to shoot in on my legs so I could sprawl, bear hug, lift, and pivot on one knee to a type of legal body slam! I went undefeated my first year in my league. I was a proud, arrogant, teenager of my accomplishments and capabilities. It kept at bay many of the potential challenges of youth. It was my last match of the season, and our team as a whole was filled with many champions of their weight class. Many of the members were wrestling AAU tournaments on weekends and had several years of experience. Our coach was skilled and trained us in many maneuvers.

I never bothered with a lot of shadow wrestling the others did. They practiced rigorously the moves before every meet. In my own mind: it was my strength. I was bench pressing two hundred and fifty pounds and had leaned down to one hundred and fifty five pounds. I was undefeated and won every match on brawn.

On to the mat, my team shouting: "SUMA! SUMA! " I take my position, although this challenge across from me looked a lot more like myself, I was confident in my strength. I would let him shoot in, roll back and body hug and turn him into a pin position! When the refs whistle blew eighteen seconds later, I was astonished, shamed, and defeated! Not just a loss, but a pin! I got pinned in eighteen seconds and my wrestling career was over! What happened? Truth happened! The truth that if you know what is coming and practiced enough counter-defensives, victory was assured! My worthy opponent had been watching me all season. I had no idea people did that at fourteen years old?

The coach and his student had been reviewing my successes as they were preparing for state finals. This was just a first year challenge for me. Who expect a first year wrestler to know all the moves... someone quick serve me some cheese with my whine! Excuses! Excuses! Excuses! I let my team down, my coach down, but mostly my pride! It wasn't my failures to fear that defeated me. It was my lack of truth. The truth that skill is in responses and reactions, as well as, foresight was to my demise. I failed to learn the truth about wrestling, that strength and endurance is important only to a point.

My opponent, despite my record, was unmoved by my historical past. He allowed his skills of truth to counter balance my moves to his victories. He went on to win state that year and I was happy to hear so.

Fear is not our obstacles. The pursuit of truth is our obstacle. We all have fears. Fear is simply the mental unknowns of life. It is understanding that fear dissolves. Most think that faith is an unknown; so, they are afraid of it. Faith should be based on truth. Everything else is just religion. People stuff! Your answer to fear is not faith yet, it is truth. It is in truth that you gain understanding. Truth is something from which you never have to back away. Truth brings rest. Truth breeds peace. Truth is security. Truth is power. It becomes confidence! Truth never has to be sold. It is given away. When truth is for sale, greed is present. This we know... "That the love of money is the root of all evil". This is the importance of education, which is professionalism at its best. When education gets corrupted by lies, it demands cover up. It becomes greed based. It becomes back door and manipulative. It generates mental decay and sociological failure. This is the history of institutional training in America. Let's create a new future by altering historical truth.

It is only in the lies of education that it self-promotes its own failures. It is the purity of truth that empowers. It is the purity of truth that employs. It is the purity of truth that discovers. It is the purity of truth that destroys tyranny! Where cover up is, tranny reigns. This is historical truth! The simple truth is that in order for truth to be truth it simply always has to be the truth. It is in the circumstantial that we bend truth. We corrupt it. We manipulate it. We infect the world. I dare you to do a reverse follow up a known lie and watch wars, death, corruption, disease, and despair evolve. Follow the history of some of the most depraved countries on the planet today, and it will expose the ugly of lie.

Exposing a lie though, is not the same as discovering truth. It is in the discovery of truth that lie exposes itself. Many people live their lies today. You can follow this through medicine. A pharmaceutical report exposed where some of the places in the United States that consume the most depression and psychotropic drugs were consumed. You will find that depression medication follows depressed economies. Following depressed economies will expose a long history of corruption.

Corruption is cover up to someone's lie. The people in these communities know the lie exists but they are too frightened and frustrated to face the truth rather than expose the lie.

It may be the lie of corruption? It may be the lie of greed? It may the lie of bullying? It may be the lie of deceits? I guarantee you though that the fear of truth is present everywhere!

As you start to seek truth and you express truth you find growth and successes follow.

Zig Ziglar taught about this in his analogies of growth: Unconsciously Unconscious to Unconsciously Conscious. He taught that we all start not knowing what we do not know. We then move to a growth point of knowing that we do not know (consciously unconscious). This is a great place to be, unless you let fear take over? To know that you do not know is where a lot of failure takes place. This is when desire kicks in. It is here that we exercise the muscle of the brain, the desires of the heart, and the appetites of growth.

When you grow past this you enter into the danger zone (consciously conscious). This where you know something about everything and you let your limited knowledge become your arrogance, or your laziness, or worse...your excuse for professionalism. When you think you know what you know is where the "ninety-percent-ers" stop growing, but, this is where the "ten-percent-ers" arise.

This is where success is bred...consciously becoming unconscious.

Every once in a while you meet genuine people; sincere, humble, people that have a desire to change the world and not just overrun the world. This is where dictators fall, generals coup, legislators negotiate, educators infect, and lawyers manipulate. To become unconscious of what we know is where truth thrives. This is humility. This is where respect permeates. This is where genuine concern explodes. Our ears become more intuitive, our mouth less destructive. When we realize our response to our circumstances preserved us from the shattered dreams, visions, and disconnected lives of others, we root ourselves in more truth. We establish truth like a building cornerstone. We lose judgment and criticisms. It is here that we offer constructive change, resolutions, and we repair breaches. We become peacemakers. We move from hourly employees to entrepreneurs. The results are more important than the time measured in dollars and cents. Not in irresponsibility, but in integrity, in equity, and in right.

This is the victory of Thomas Edison. Not in the failed attempts of making a light bulb, but the successes in learning how not to make a light bulb! We move from mediocre to masters.

We propel into motion the senses of faith, not just dead or exhausting work! Not just business or 'busyness', but accomplishment. We do not turn back on truth. We forge forward in truth. It is in truth that if time continues we will populate the universe; discover new worlds; new ways; more truth! We have conquered fear. Truth is absolute. Truth is not circumstantial. Truth is unmovable. Truth is resolve.

It is in truth that we conquer all other obstacles. Truth shall set you free.

Fear is indecisiveness. Fear is the instability of grey. Fear is refusal to learn. There is an inability to choose right, when there is an absence of information. We cannot make decisions on half- truths and incomplete flow of information. This only creates confusion, frustration, and more fear. We should search for truth like a treasure and we would gain wisdom beyond our years. If we would take the time to recognize truth in its equity, it would become our number one pursuit.

Many were sold the American dream; that roses grew freely on every street corner, right next to the bubble plants and the money trees! Many forgot to mention that the roses were constantly under attack by June beetles, the bubbles burst in the wind, and that money trees were leased by the government and haven't budded in 50 years. This is not pessimism, this is misinformation.

Success comes before work, only in the dictionary. Every once in a while it appears that some strange phenomenon of a pet rock shows itself. I do not believe it is an unplanned event. Facebook is not a freak, Facebook was a need; a need of communication and connection. I believe it has its draw backs and has open many up to another addiction and failure to communicate. What an oxymoron? It is not a coincidence though. It was thought out. It was strategic. It filled a niche, too say the least. But its success has been based on a truth, a simple need to connect lives. It is just a public diary of too much information some times, but all in all, it is the convenience of sharing a thought, a hope, a prayer, a laugh, a cut, a picture, a pet peeve, condemnation, or a simple memory of life. This year there will be another and next yet another. It is though a rarity. A rarity that someone thinks through, follows through, and overcomes the phony obstacles of excuses, procrastination, and fears to accomplish the next step toward the establishment of truth.

I once was shared a truth, that people wanted to be heard more than talked to or about. It was in this simple truth that many successes were born. That if I heard what was said I could respond with an opportunity to resolve. It is in resolve that the resolute of truth lives.

I developed an acrostic: "H.E.R.O.".

> **H**ear what is said.

> **E**mpathize with what you heard.

> **R**educe and respond in clarification.

> **O**vercome the obstacle with opportunity to resolve.

So, I learned how always to be the hero!

This catapulted my sales through several industries. Many would hear about my successes and ask if they could ride with me for a day or teach a class or share an inspiration. What many would not realize is that my successes were not the things I said; the catchy phrase or quip that all could use as the key to their personal treasure chest. It was what I heard that generated millions in sales. I would ask simple questions about themselves and their concerns and then shut my mouth and listen. It was in listening that truth was exposed or lies checkmated. Someone once gave me a compliment that I considered the greatest condemnation. They said; "Jeff, you could sell screen doors to submarine commanders". I chuckled when I first heard that. After contemplation, I prayed that no one would ever say that about me again. I didn't want to sell anybody anything that they didn't need or didn't want. I wanted to sleep at night and I do very well. I decided that if I could not be truthful about what I did, sold, or encouraged others to get involved in that I would not do it! "So, let me make sure I understand you correctly, if you could have this or that without it interfering with this or that, then we would be able to do business today?" I simply listened to what was potentially expected and then delivered what was asked. I never had to sell anything. I just supplied needs based on their truths they shared. Sometimes people aren't honest...and that is a truth we all have to understand.

Bill Gothard, once said, "Persuasiveness is guiding vital truths around another person's mental roadblocks." I am not as good a chess player as I would like to be, but I love the term "checkmate".

As I said earlier, Truth is something of which you do not have to be afraid. It brings peace and confidence. I was brought to truth at many different times throughout my life, that "Come to Jesus" expression. Truth always does that. It comes to be recognized. It demands understanding. We get reproved in it. It grows us.

In midsummer of 2012, my youngest daughter was diagnosed with Acute Lymphoblastic Leukemia. Her being born with Downs Syndrome was the first obstacle of her life. When her infantile spasms started, it complicated the obstacles. We arose victorious over these obstacles in truth. The many thoughts of things to fear arose. The overwhelming thoughts of what -when and who -how and why-this and me-oh-my, my wife and I, took some hard punches. As the unofficial diagnosis came in about the leukemia, my wife did not understand what the resident was saying. I had to explain their implications. Whatever was ahead she needed some hemoglobin. With the hemoglobin, was then needed platelets. With the platelets was then needed anti-biotic. With the anti-biotic was then needed anti-diarrhea and electrolytes. It was a vicious cycle of balances and trade-off side effects.

When the hospital got more suspicious of it being Leukemia, they got more intense about starting chemotherapy. We felt like we are at a vacuum sales meeting at someone else's house and they would not let us go until we bought something. I have never been more railroaded and disrespected in all my life. Let alone threatened, bullied, and hoodwinked. Believe me, my daughter's life was our greatest concern. I do not know who was getting the bonus for us to sign the document of no return, but there appeared several in the running? Despite the circumstance, truth was the only calm. I may not be able to change our current events, but I became resolved that if we were going to have to cross this bridge that I would do everything in my capabilities to make it better for the next to have to pass this way! It was in this truth that I documented everything; names, times, events, conversations, and observations. No family should ever have to be treated this way, especially in the concerns of these avenues.

My daughter did not understand her violations? My entire being was challenged. I went to patient advocacy to only find they were paid staff of the hospital. That is like going to the mafia and telling them their insurance is too costly! It was somewhat entertaining to document statements and events and ask with a "Colombo accent" "let me understand you if I may?" Only to get condescension, more lies, and cover up as the average response. But it was the consistency of truth that allowed me to gather.

It was not so much that our daughter may have leukemia, but it was how we were forced to address it. The 14th amendment was never written to this group. One doctor said," Mr. Jones, there is no miracle on this planet that will get your daughter out of my intent to give her chemo!" I was called out! He might as well said, "Would you like to step out in the alley?"

I kept picturing these giant banners that read: "HOPE", "INSPIRE", "BELIEVE" that hung braggadocios from the hallways entering the compound.

I didn't get that in the statement from the doctor, nor an apology yet as the typing of these pages. I am avowed to correct this travesty. I was not being driven by an attack on the standards of care as much as

I was being challenged in a truth that miracles do not exist. My faith was being attacked to generate my fear. But fear is not an obstacle, truth is! Albert Einstein said;" If you judge a fish for its ability to climb a tree, it will believe its whole life that it is stupid." This is what fear does!

So as I gather truth and share that truth, fear gets defeated. This will get exposed in other arenas, I can assure you! So as fear stands dark and looming, I turn to truth. So CPS was falsely directed to question. Not my intents of release of our daughter, but that they were told by a doctor that our daughter had never been seen by a physician for her Downs? Like Downs was something curable? She was born in a hospital. She was born with Downs. She had no other medical conditions at the time of her birth.

She developed these spams later of which we took her to see the "World Renown Specialist" located near our home in a prominent hospital. He told us there was no cure. That the medicines they had in the states were extremely ineffective and that the side effects were in the highest percentiles to cause blindness, kidney damage, and serious cognitive disabilities for life. We expressed our concerns in his diagnoses and did what we always do...PRAY! We prayed for guidance, directional, intervention, and resolve. Within one week her spasms ceased. We added some supplements and essential oils to the day and it has been six years free of what the "World Specialist" said was incurable!

So when a few hematologists and PA's tell us how they our going to command the helm of death management, we have our concerns as genuine loving parents. But it has been truth that has carried us through this night mere of attacks. Selah's blast count went from 47 to 3 in ten days and without chemo! Suspiciously, the zero appeared within 40 hours of her first treatment. Something that was referred to as a "Phenomenon", in one report!

We were forced into protocols, but we have done everything possible to restore life into our daughter in this battle. We are Life managers. We are truth seekers. We do not fear death. Truth tells us, we pass from death to life! This truth reflects our faith. This faith is simply the exercising of truth.

Innocence cannot be judged and judgment was already served! After 2 years of continued chemo on a body that has been undetectable of cancer is a crime against humanity that demands notice!

As we became exhausted, and the ugliest of moments as our little girls life was someone else's medical experiment of poisons and protocol that of which we were being held captive, truth sustained us. I knelt on the floor one night next to Selah's hospital bed, again not because of cancer, but because of side effects forced upon her little body, I cried and asked a merciful Creator to come into the room, into this wing, on to the 7th floor, and show himself strong. I pleaded and said, if you would just step into the room, everything would be alright. I waited for a moment in anticipation of a mighty wind, or some mysterious voice, but it didn't come. Something more life changing, more solidifying, a deeper truth emerged. In the stillness of my wait, a peace overwhelmed my soul! No, a truth overcame my obstacles!

Jeff, if you believe what you believe, where do you think I am right now? I broke into tears in the realization that HE was already there, he never left me, for he dwells with in me. **TRUTH LIVES IN ME!**

It was then that the truth that I never knew this world existed here on the 7th floor all over the world. That although aware of diseases, tragedies, and heart ache, here was a group of people living hopeless on this globe and somewhere encouragement and reconciliation was going to have to take place. A foundation was being born.

This would overtake the next year of living and targeting. That even though I was able to take two years from work to tend to my family, many could not, that these events are catastrophic; financially, spiritually, socially, and structurally. That a single parent trying to manage these events around getting other children to school, work, and or other life events; could completely disable hope.

Hearing, seventy percent of marriages fail inside of this travesty is devastating information. Going through this though, brings complete understanding. Understanding brings resolve. Resolve is truth upon equation. I may not be able to change protocols but I can help change the experiences of protocol. I believe there are alternatives to traditional medicines. That preventative is always better then reactionary or emergency.

That is education, and education should always be truth, and never manipulation and cover up, remember? Pharmaceuticals, Associations, Government, and Administrators help manipulate business into selective banks. That profitability is now the resounding direction of medicine.

This is not an attempt to stereotype. This is just the simple truth that greed exists in every crevice of this terrestrial. That we do not fight medicine, but the accounting principles of administration have to be closely observed. Like a piece of cheese at a rodent's convention, everyone wants the same dollar. The research labs, the universities, the WHO, the military, the FDA, the AMA, ACS, the charities, and the businesspeople, all like a fiend in a crack house justifying their thievery. Remember again, that if you find any deep deprivation, there is always a deep root.

It is the fulfilment of the account recorded in the book of John chapter eight with emphasis on verse thirty two and forty four. All the way through chapter 14 there is a recurring direction of truth that transcends time. It is only an excerpt and recap of the rest of the 7000 years of history recorded from cover to cover, awaiting the ultimate truth of Einstein's theory. (Unfortunately, Albert's ideas are only relative on earth inside the confines of our known limited physical laws.)

Here is the paradox, that the eternals are actually defined. That physics get defied daily and that miracles are a truth outside of man's understandings. May we call this, the spiritual? Yet God asks us to worship him in spirit and in truth. This is where religion gets divided, man's concept and the Creators design. It was in this truth that the cycle of my daughter's battle was exposed.

I sat one night rocking her to sleep as I always do, and in her stillness she lay. I was conquered by the truth how GOD experiences us. I could not interfere with my daughter's circumstance. I could only comfort her through it. Because my daughter does not communicate in quite the same manner, up until just recently, she never could say, "I love you". For the first years of her life, she was almost emotionless. She hadn't cried. She rarely smiled. She had not recognized us as her caring parents. As the expressions of pain, neurological damage, and sickness overtook her, all I could do is love her through it.

This conflict taught me the truth of godliness. That despite him ever hearing the words, ever being noticed as a giver of life, for all the things that he did protect us from, for every provision of design we did enjoy, he did this regardless of our responses. This is how he loves. This is how he rolls. Not needing the acknowledgement, the kudos, the accolades, he did what he did. He does what he does. He is who he is. He will always be, the same yesterday, today, and forever; truth in his eternals, not having to justify to me the why's or the how's or the why not's. Yet, when I do acknowledge this, he brings me favor. He delivers. He upholds. He rescues. He recovers. He fortifies. He fights for us and defends us. He is the," I AM"! The Alpha and Omega! The Almighty! The Allah! The Elohim! The Resurrection! The Light! Straight up take me down bring me up, the AMEN, The Truth!

CHAPTER 3

In Absentia:

Much like there is no such thing as cold or no such thing as dark, there is no such thing as ignorance or indecisiveness. Now we know that we have all experienced ignorance, dark and cold. Yet, cold is just the absence of heat and dark is just the absence of light. Maybe we could look at many opposites in the same way? Wrong is the absence of right? Ugly is the absence of beauty? By the way, beauty is more an attitude than it is a physical presence! Is not then evil the absence of good? So also, ignorance and indecisiveness is just the absence of information. There are three basic characters of the book of Proverbs: the wise; the simple; and the fool. The wise seeks truth and its source. The simple is unaware of these, while the fool ignores it all together. The source of information or the truth that created it makes it viable and constructive. If somebody receives misinformation, obviously, one would draw a different conclusion, they have become misguided. Certainly without a bearing, a point of origin, a Greenwich Village, or a North Star, direction can be misinterpreted quite easily.

Right and left become situational.

When in all essence, right is always right, and left is always left, if from the same perspective. A treasure map is worthless without a point of reference.   Truth is the exact same way. If my origin is without observations, hypothesis, and study, then it is simply not scientific or teachable as theory at least. If it is taught as truth, when it does not qualify with the means of equation, then it is a complete attack on the genius of humankind. Sometimes the evidence is all the same, but it is interpreted by our own past or historical experiences. This could be scars, fears, and or situational circumstances that cause us to come to a different resolve. That is why Proverbs 4:23 tell us to 'Guard our hearts, for out of it are the issues of life'. We can choose anything we want as an individual and even more so as an American.

Yet, we cannot choose the consequences of our choices. It is in the accumulation of truth that these damages become less often and less destructive. As our heart scars or our mind remembers, we may rethink our choices? These are the miseries of youth, unless we learn wisdom beyond our years? If we seek truth like a hid treasure we discover greater. Proverbs 8:12 encourages us to follow prudent thinking and discernment. This leads to creativity. Creativity leads to invention. Inventions can lead to prosperity, here in America especially! This was the Renaissance. This also was the Industrial Revolution.

This was the day of the silicon chip, fax, cell phone, and PC. This is part of the American dream. This is why we still have thousands of people daily trying to move here to live from all over the world. I haven't heard lately, people trying to rush into North Korea because they have an invention, an idea, or intellectual property that will create their personal prosperity. Could it be the pursuit of a higher truth that brings people from all over the world to the U.S.? Is it the truth of a constitution that allows, "We the people", to think ; to pursue; to believe?

Is it then the resolve of the founding fathers that created intent of truth in the pursuit of happiness?

That the terminology, "One Nation, Under GOD, Indivisible, with liberty and justice for all" had an origin?

That we have lost something from Black's Law and the New England Primer? Or that Harvard was originally a school of divinity? Or in early American history that you had to have a theological degree before you could hold public office? Or how that at fourteen years of age John Quincy Adams served as part of a diplomatic team that went to Russia? Can you imagine today a teenager being part of our Secretary of State? This is just to show the decay of truth! How far have we come in today's society to even identify truth? Have we been blinded to truth? Is it not the fact that we respond to what we think we see and very rarely do we take time to discover truth? I read it in the papers, or saw it on CNN, or heard it on FOX, I got an email, or someone shared a Facebook? I remember as a young teen I bought my own subscription to U.S. News and World Report. My father was a Time/Life and Newsweek man. I even remember growing up with the old LOOK magazine. One day I was asking my father some questions about world affairs. He had a different story then I had about the whole event. I couldn't understand why my dad didn't have the same perspective and concerns about this event as myself? I then decided to read through his collections of" toiletries", things he read in the bathroom. I could not believe what I saw? The same pictures had different captions? The same headlines had a different story?

I was astonished? I was naïve? I was confused and interrupted! I was being educated in a truth.

As so Lucifer, being the first of creation, the bringer of light, was sent on a quest to observe and absorb. I see truth as a circle. As he pursued truth in its entirety, half way around the circumference of the universe, it was discovered in truth that if I am bigger I may be able to overtake, overrun, or conquer if you please, my weaker interactions. So Lu, discovering a truth that misinformation, a lie, may cover the truth? This was a new concept in truth on this journey. That there were other truths of physics, opposition, and war that could lead to a personal victory were all now being uncovered. Unfortunately, this is a truth that wrong can sometimes overtake right. In the innocence of youth, naivety, (lack of information discovered), can be over powered or misled. Once innocence is robbed it cannot ever be restored. This is another fragile truth. I remember innocence, the sweet unburdened beautiful carelessness of not knowing. This was the fall of humankind. The truth of origin in a garden that was designed to accommodate our forever, unburdened by sweat, pain, heartache, sickness, disease, loneliness, disparity, depravity, death, and untruth. This was paradise.

Although having boundaries, complete freedom and carefree relation with a generous loving Creator. All was ours to enjoy, and if full filled, an ever expanding universe to populate. One rule and one rule only, don't eat of the tree of knowledge of good and evil. But it sounds so admirable to know the difference?

So, as the story goes obviously, we ate. This was the gift of choice! You can choose anything you want; you just cannot choose the consequences of your choices. So humankind chose to make their own decisions, rather than having Truth and Perfection make choices for them. This has proven itself complete calamity. Good still exists, truth still reigns, we just now have to seek it, to obtain it. We call this degeneration. Time has spoken clearly and money talks loudly, maybe this is why so many are actually silent? We have no time because we are too busy trying to make money. The greatest oxymoron on the planet is the term labeled to our money; "In God We Trust". The perfect lie, the perfect discovery, the perfect hiding place, the perfect cover up, in broad view for all to see!

Novus Ordo Seclorum!

Annuit Ceoptus.

The Federal Reserve <u>NOTE</u>...the perfect lying debt instrument for the world to grope after. I may spend more time on it; If not in this collection of words, certainly another.

I started to search other papers and periodicals on the same subject and found different points of origin! In my pursuit, I discovered that truth was the only origin of which I was interested.

That despite different perspectives there was always a truth to define. That right and wrong although clouded by grey was eventually distinguishable.

I was traveling on an airplane one day and the ground was cold and icy. The gray haze of the freezing rain and winter storm waiting to brew was stifling. I was concerned about delays and turbulent winds. As the plane lifted from the ground, it shook and rocked. It was as though the very wings were going to snap off. We rose into the dark gray and it was worse. The lightening flashed and the immense density of clouds was completely blinding. The gray became white and the clouds began to thin as we rocketed on through this unknown mass. Then, like the break of day, the sun was clear as a shimmering daystar and the sky as blue as an Aruban ocean! This was more truth!

From my ground perspective I could only see the gray. From my new perspective, the sky was bright and beautiful blue! The truth hadn't changed. The sky was always blue. It really wasn't my perspective that made the sky blue. The sky was always as it is, blue! So, despite the storms, the clouds, the current events of our lives, the circumstances if you please, the sky is always blue above it all! Thus, "Mr. Blue Skies", became a beautiful identification for me. So I had to focus on what I did not see. Like a pilot flying VFR, I had to learn to trust the indicators.

One of my favorite stories about perspective comes from a familiar story about a child watching her grandmother do embroidery from the carpet view of the play area. "Grandma", the child inquired, "What a mess you are making". "Be patient child" she kindly replied. "But Grandma, the strings the overlapping colors, the mess of entanglement...it looks awful!" "Be patient child"; Grandma kindly replied. Insistently, the child pursued, "Grandma, what a waste of time to tie all those knots and strands of dangling strings?" Come child" Grandma motioned. "Get on my lap". As the child climbed up she was amazed at the most beautiful intricate array of colors to a picture perfect scene of garden flowers and birdsong! This again is truth, that when we view from the right origin, we get definition, and confusion and loose ends vanish into well planned order, much like our big beautiful universe. This is the diaspora of world view.

I dislike the questions of identification on government forms and other miscellaneous ones that ask to identify race, origin, or religion? There is only one race, humankind! We all came from our mother, did we not?

Others would like you to think otherwise, but there really are only two religions on the whole of creation; the DO religion and the DONE religion. The DO religion says you have to do something to merit paradise, heaven, peace, or eternity.

The DONE religion recognizes it is complete. You only have to accept the truth of it. I will go even one step further and say all religion is the same there is only one, what humankind creates.

Whether atheistic, agnostic or evangelistic, if it is human created, directed, and governed, it is religion.

It is the origin of truth that only changes. MY life motto of Life, Love Acceptance, and Forgiveness, (LLAF as an acrostic), is not judgmental, condemning, overpowering, or condescending.

This is the core of truth. As a respecter of life and not of personage, I become an advocate for living.

As I stand in the position of love, it is my obligation to provide the necessities of living to others without making gain of them in the process. With the truth of acceptance, I continue in genuine love, not expecting someone to be who I need them to be or think or look or act or respond in my view of normalcy, but rather treating as myself how would I like to be treated? Lastly, forgiveness was given to me through grace and grace is what I need to offer others. Never to live or respond in revenge, but react with forgiveness and understanding that I too once did not know truth.

Now though, I am accountable to it! Simply put, "Love thy neighbor as thyself".

So establishing that truth is not situational, manipulated, or circumstantial, these are the misdirection's of fear or faithlessness. Here is another truth. The presence of fear is the absence of faith. We will address faith in the coming chapters, and this is not religiosity. Fear is the driving force behind the unknown. Unknown demands discovery. Discovery is knowledge. Knowledge is power only in understanding. Confusion is not having understanding. Thus, confusion is the absence or twisting of truth. Why do you think insurance contracts, warranties, and guarantees are confusing?

Because they try to mask truth! This is a form of cover up.

Remember cover up leads to more fear and more decay, and eventually depression and despair. Insurance is truthful, but many of the truths do not want to be discovered. Most are manipulated into insurance. Insurance can be an asset and not always a liability, but the truth of it must be explained. Understanding must be solidified in order for this to be ethical.

It is in the process of ethics that we establish truth. Here we are again in this paradox. Truth is measured in degrees. Three hundred and sixty degrees make a full circle. Truth is a whole circle.

is this paradox. Truth is the ethical standard. If it is a half-truth, it becomes a whole lie! In order for truth to be truth, it simply has to always be the truth. Truth is not circumstantial.

We may argue gun control is the way to resolve another Columbine, or Connecticut, or Virginia Tech? Would we actually stop violence with more gun control or lower violent crimes? If we didn't make guns, no one would ever die from a gunshot. Yet, this not the truth about teenage suicides, school yard shootings, or gang bangs.

Last week some foundation donation jars were stolen again, from the Selah Says Society. Let us say this happened all at a chain of locations under the same name, but different physical locations. So the corporate headquarters issues a regulation that their stores will no longer allow donation jars to be placed in their stores, thus eliminating never to have jars stolen ever again! Or this happens in a particular city in different locations, so the city issues a law that no donation jars are allowed in their city. This is the thinking of today's policy makers.

True that you will never have donation jars stolen, but have you eliminated stealing?

Do you make laws that attack right or charity sincerity because of the abuse or lack of ethic and truth in ones upbringing? This is not resolve, this a placebo, a panacea!

This is making truth circumstantial. It wears it down and masquerades the real. This again is cover up.

So, in the same likeness, do we outlaw guns for the criminal or for the protectorate? I agree with gun control regulations, but certainly not confiscation of an Americans right to keep and bear arms!

Thomas Jefferson — 'When the people fear the government there is tyranny, when the government fears the people there is liberty.

Herein is today's politician. Nothing is ever a lie: it is simply the absence of truth? We didn't vote for that, we just didn't show up when it was time to vote to stop it. Or it was voted in by default, 'I personally couldn't make it that day'?

Remember, cover up is a lie usually based on greed or pride that leads to depression and depravity.

CHAPTER 4

Why Six Thousand Miles To The Liffey And Rye?

I went on a mission trip to Ireland. I was actually recommended not to go by some deciduous. I kept hearing about kids being blown up in car bombings or street wars. I kept praying that GOD would intervene and send somebody to bring resolve.

After several weeks of listening to the BBC, I got on my knees in tears, and said GOD please stop this madness. Raise someone up that could make a difference.

I got up off my knees and God said; "Why not you?" "Why not me… what?" You talking… to me! " Jeff, you go" "I can't go! I have a family, no money in the budget, and I am nobody." He said," You are somebody though".

So I called the local travel agent and asked how much was a flight to Belfast. The number that came back was beyond my wildest expectation. "So OK, I'm not going to Northern Ireland."

The next day the travel agent called up and asked if I still wanted to go to Ireland. I said "yes"! I didn't have that kind of money ($2800). She said," Do you have $200?" I said yes but why? She said a major company had a chartered flight into Shannon, Ireland that somehow had open seats that they wanted to fill to offset some contract and if I had $200 I could fly into Shannon. The only glitch was that was not Northern Ireland nor I could not specify when I could go nor when I could return? The flight would be at will and at least 10 days apart from return.

I agreed and went.

Landing in Shannon, I called a friend of a friend in Dublin. Seeing that Dublin was a mere 150 kilometers away, I would be there in a leisurely three hour drive? Eight hours later, I reached my destination. Right sided driving on the left side of the road took a bit getting acquainted.

Also, my first encounter with a round-a-bout! I arrived just in time to see the country side covered in signs about the "Lilywhites"? Left handed shifting in a MICRA was going to be a chore!?!

I hadn't even talked to anyone and many times I had heard; "Stupid American"? I finally figured it was those round-a-bouts that got me driving on the wrong side of the road, one time through a construction area for several miles. This is a great way to get out of traffic jams in Ireland and it is amazing how many people are so kind to foreigners who exit on to the shoulder while driving on their side of the road at seventy kilometers an hour!

I was lost heading into Lixlip and worn out by all the people hollering and waving at me?!? I finally stopped a country gentleman on bicycle to get directions to Captain's Way. He quickly identified me as an American, breathed something under his breath in Gaelic, and kindly pointed me into the opposite directions of my destination. I can imagine that was quite the wink and nod as he lit his pipe after dinner that day! Making my destination, I would stay within walking distance of the Guinness Castle.

I could have stayed in the Republic for a long time! I had no idea Ireland had palm trees? Not sure if I could eat black pudding again, now knowing what it is? I eventually headed into Belfast after finding a family that was victimized by a family members shooting.

I arrived on a Sunday evening into Northern Ireland. It was quite the contrast from the Republics east coast drive. Twelve foot steel walls surrounding a city with Dannert wire wrapped heavily around its top, was not what I expected. There are absolutely beautiful places all over the country; I just did not expect to see what I saw? I made my way to the comforts of the Braehill Baptist Church for evening service. They were sending missionaries into London. The country that one day launched more missionaries around the globe than anywhere else, was now in need of truth being replenished into a land covered in cover up and insurrection. What a twist?!

After the generous comforts of fellowship and contact and I was informed that I needed to take a holiday. The one that was going to show me around Belfast had some other priorities and asked if had anything I would like to do. I quickly responded; "The Giants Causeway"! So off I go on an early Monday morning up to Bushmills. Arriving early, to make a good day on the Irish Sea, I stopped for breakfast. Like a picture out of a Thomas Kinkade collection, this nestled little village with world renown was picturesque! I enjoyed my breakfast and the community was quite friendly, until I went to pay for my meal. I place my money on the table and the waitress stomps off into the back room and big burly cook steps out of the kitchen, with the brogue of an Irish sailor, "Ya notbe payin' for y'ur breakfast with that kind of money ron' here!" I explained that I was just up from the Republic and had no time to exchange from Punt to Sterling. He sternly replies;" YA sit rite dare, n wait'il da banks open ta get'che'rself sum proper money!" (translation emphasis).

So the banks open, I walk across the circle and exchange my punt for sterling. I came back and pay my bill and the cook smiles with the warmest of kindness; "Now have yourself a lovely holiday!" I smirk as I walk to the door and remind myself I am the stranger.

Making all this fuss, a handful of elder fisherman and gad-about, were congregated waiting to give an evil eye or a nod? When I came out smiling, they scattered?

The scenery was ripe, quaint, and mysterious. The 'mourning' fog was lifting as I gazed around the square. One man left holding his bicycle is all that remained and a faint swirling of the mist as the rest had since scattered into Coventry? I noticed the graffiti that said "'We shoot police tout"? I also noticed a flag high flying in circled center of the town square, a plain white flag with a deep red hand and crown.

I asked the lingering gentleman about this flag with that I was so unfamiliar. My voice shattered the silence, and he harshly replied' "That be the bloody hand Ulster"! I again was unmoved by the attempt at shivering me along. He explains," There was a Scottish Chieftain that had ownership of the land of Ulster. He had two sons. He decided to host a race that would determine the heir to this land. The Chieftain explained that they would race across the Irish Sea and whoever would touch the shore first would be declared the winner and reward. The two sons jump in their vessels and race across the violence of the waters to shores of their target. They both arrive at the same time and lunge their craft into the banks. The one brother looking at his possible defeat, quickly pulls out his sword, chops off his hand, and throws his own bloodied hand onto the shore before his brother steps foot. Thus, winning the race! How true I will not dare doubt otherwise, but that is exactly how the story came to me.

When returning to Belfast, I would find even more to the story. With a street corner painted red, white, and blue and the opposite painted green, white, and orange, the boundaries were set. Unlike the Crypts and Bloods of Detroit, or any other gang in the metropolitans of the world, these were paramilitary combat units with rocket launcher gang insignias! The conflict would end if a winner would be declared. The story the man told me in Bushmill was now so clear. You never call an Irishman a cheat! But rather, how far would you go to defame yourself to be called the winner?

This is the truth of the conflict in my observations. All the ugly, the terror, the depravity, and the disaster, is the result of the ugly of lie, scandal, and cover up. Having roots to the oldest Jones clan of Ireland, I only wish I knew better. Here on this magnificent rock of green, song, and glee, is the rotting truth that someone can always be more outrageous than you. What a crime against the Christ that represents both sides. This again is called degeneration.

This, is truth that had led to abuse that had denied its empowering head to crown. St. Patrick, The Church, the Orangeman, and Banshee what a picture perfect view in the decays of truth! This is humanity. This is religiosity. This is Government. This is pride. This is the lie. This is the venture around the circle. This is the Palestinian conflict. This is Gaza. This is the Taliban. This is Pakistan. This is Afghanistan. This is Bosnia. This is Egypt. This is the Sudan. This is the LRA. This was Mogadishu. This was Armenia. This was the Holocaust. This was the Spanish Inquisition. This was the Crusades. This is the covering and manipulation of truth! This is my passion! Two wrongs do not make a right!

JAMES 4:1 From whence come wars and fightings among you? Come they not hence, even of your lusts that war in your members? [2] Ye lust, and have not: ye kill, and desire to have, and cannot obtain: ye fight and war, yet ye have not, because ye ask not. [3] Ye ask, and receive not, because ye ask amiss, that ye may consume it upon your lusts.

CHAPTER 5

<u>Doubt is Bad Fortune Telling</u>

Doubt is bad fortune telling. The full impact of doubt is disabling. Doubt says stop all engines. Doubt is the not even real. It is simply a mental gastritis. It is made of two key components, experience and ignorance. These are also the two primary components of faith, as well. This is not coincidence. This is by design. Not the design of a masterful creator, but the design of the ultimate deceiver. Doubt is simply the ignorance of truth. It is either the stubbornness to refuse what you would like to believe or the complete insubordination that God has no idea about what he is talking. Our historical experiences can speak loudly or softly. Just because you experienced one result does not mean everyone else experience the same. This is the birthing grounds of skepticism. Skepticism says we are all doomed, the essentials of hopelessness. Hopelessness is the absence of faith. So doubt is just a non-real position of the mind to refuse hope.

Nearly two thousand years ago it was written, "I can do all things through Christ which strengthens me."

Even the incompleteness of metaphysics this truth permeates all beings. When you come to the recognition the one who breathed all things into existence, consists in you, this becomes complete empowerment. Impossible is the limited sight of humankind into the completeness of creation.

I spoke of origin in earlier chapters. If you have a different prime meridian then I, we will only by miraculous chance land at the same destination. The route is not in any way connective. We are on the same planet, but living in different worlds. It is in the absolute that I find my peace and refuge. Not that I do not question. It is the questioning that we find the root word, "Quest". There is no quest in doubt. No adventure! No destination! No hope!

So let's move this into truth. So Chris Columbus comes up with this doubt, that the world is a sphere? Do you see the ridiculousness of this? So maybe Tom Edison says I doubt if electricity can be harnessed? Maybe, Hank Ford says, " I doubt we can ever get more product, lower costs, or be more effective?"

So to say I doubt there is a heaven. Or to say I doubt there is a God? Or even to say, "I doubt I could ever hope", is the depravity of thought, science, creativity, adventure, and what I have come to call, "LIVING". So, we would rather say, "I don't have all the facts", "I have yet to have that experience", or "I simply choose not to believe". Ignorance is the lack of knowledge, understanding, information, experience, or tried results. Insubordination is the refusal to accept the facts, tests, historical, documented, results. Has anyone ever been successful? Is everyone successful? Does everyone have the same passion, vision, dreams, or appetites? Has anyone ever made a million dollars? Has anyone ever crossed the ocean? Has anyone ever walked the moon? Has anyone ever conquered a nation? Has an underdog ever won?

 Has anyone ever been created something new? Let me ask you this... has the impossible ever been? With great enthusiasm, exuberance, and unbounded passion..."OFCOURSE"! So, is doubt your final answer? Is doubt the perspective in which you want to live? Is doubt the end of your adventures? Or is doubt the inception that someone else or something else wants of you? A physician once wrote, "...with God all things are possible"! Now, that would be a miraculous change of conception.

Has anyone ever been wrong about the future? An amazing historical story about a deceitful man named Jacob is a great reminder. Jacob cheats his brother and deceives his elderly father, completely unethical! He then takes advantage of a moment of carelessness and gets his brother to surrender his legacy, swindles his brothers trust documents, if you please! He then, abandons his family for fear of his life. He in turn, gets hoodwinked buy his father-in-law several times. Then, disappearing into the night with his belongings, someone's daughters (his wives), someone's grandchildren (his own kids), and again abandoning a family corporation, he gets homesick!?! On the journey and though many years later, he sends gifts before him to hopefully buy his brothers love and families respect.

 Fortunately, in the wee of the dark, the edge of the wilderness of life, he wrestles in petition with his maker. Not letting go until he begs for freedom, forgiveness, and favor, the sun rises with the scars of a warrior. Out of joint, worn, and humbled, he stands a prince with God. Blessed and favored in a land that flowed with milk and honey, he continues his prosperous journey.

As his sons grow, his community falters. In the jealousy of a favored half-brother, his son, Jo, has a falling out with his siblings.

They sell him to a traveling trade show and deceive their father that his son is dead. 'And he (Jacob) knew it, and said, it is my son's coat; an evil beast has eaten him up, Lil' Joey, is without a doubt... vultures fodder'. Although the facts presented were a lie, they appeared as without hope! But oh what a story of faith, courage, resolve, destiny, and amazement, when Lil' Jo grows up to be,"Zapnathpeneah", "Savior of the World"!

This story is found in Genesis 37, just one of thousands, recorded events of the impossible just for the doubter to simply change their thought process; to get out of the confines of the unreality of their mental barriers.

This is the design of a merciful Maker. When all looked lost, faith arose victorious! Never take the promises of God as a doubtful dispensation of his truth. Faith is an individual adventure. It does not belong to one group or another. It cannot be contained in denominationalism. It cannot be fulfilled until exercised. Like a muscle, it can be strengthened! What appears impossible, ridiculous, and even border insanity, is an individual's right to exercise their faith! Something only allowed now in America, and that is finally under attack. A chief justice said, 'The Bill of Rights, the freedom of religion is something the United States can no longer afford.' This is the destiny of doubt. This is the insubordination of humanity.

This is the ignorance of the doubter.

Romans 1:[16] For I am not ashamed of the gospel of Christ: for it is the power of God unto salvation to everyone that believeth; to the Jew first, and also to the Greek.[17] For therein is the righteousness of God revealed from faith to faith: as it is written, The just shall live by faith.[18] For the wrath of God is revealed from heaven against all ungodliness and unrighteousness of men, who hold the truth in unrighteousness;[19] Because that which may be known of God is manifest in them; for God hath shewed it unto them.[20] For the invisible things of him from the creation of the world are clearly seen, being understood by the things that are made, even his eternal power and Godhead; so that they are without excuse:[21] Because that, when they knew God, they glorified him not as God, neither were thankful; but became vain in their imaginations, and their foolish heart was darkened.[22] Professing themselves to be wise, they became fools,[23] And changed the glory of the uncorruptible God into an image made like to corruptible man, and tobirds, and fourfooted beasts, and creeping things.[24] Wherefore God also gave them up to uncleanness through the lusts of their own hearts, to dishonour their own bodies between themselves:[25] Who changed the truth of God into a lie, and worshipped and served the creature more than the Creator, who is blessed forever. Amen.[26] For this cause God gave them up unto vile affections: for even their women did change the natural use into that which is against nature:[27] And likewise also the men, leaving the natural use of the woman, burned in their lust one another; men with men working that which is unseemly, and receiving in themselves that recompence of their error which was meet.[28] And even as they did not like to retain God in their knowledge, God gave them over to a reprobate mind, to do those things which are not convenient;[29] Being filled with all unrighteousness, fornication, wickedness, covetousness, maliciousness; full of envy, murder, debate, deceit, malignity; whisperers,[30] Backbiters, haters of God, despiteful, proud, boasters, inventors of evil things, disobedient to parents,[31] Without understanding, covenant-breakers, without natural affection, implacable, unmerciful:[32] Who knowing the judgment of God, that they which commit such things are worthy of death, not only do the same, but have pleasure in them that do them.

Hebrews 11: 1 Now faith is the substance of things hoped for, the evidence of things not seen.[2] For by it the elders obtained a good report.[3] Through faith we understand that the worlds were framed by the word of God, so that things which are seen were not made of things which do appear.[4] By faith Abel offered unto God a more excellent sacrifice than Cain, by which he obtained witness that he was righteous, God testifying of his gifts: and by it he being dead yet speaketh.[5] By faith Enoch was translated that he should not see death; and was not found, because God had translated him: for before his translation he had this testimony, that he pleased God.[6] But without faith it is impossible to please him: for he that cometh to God must believe that he is, and that he is a rewarder of them that diligently seek him.[7] By faith Noah, being warned of God of things not seen as yet, moved with fear, prepared an ark to the saving of his house; by the which he condemned the world, and became heir of the righteousness which is by faith.[8] By faith Abraham, when he was called to go out into a place which he should after receive for an inheritance, obeyed; and he went out, not knowing whither he went.[9] By faith he sojourned in the land of promise, as in a strange country, dwelling in tabernacles with Isaac and Jacob, the heirs with him of the same promise:[10] For he looked for a city which hath foundations, whose builder and maker is God.[11] Through faith also Sara herself received strength to conceive seed, and was delivered of a child when she was past age, because she judged him faithful who had promised.[12] Therefore sprang there even of one, and him as good as dead, so many as the stars of the sky in multitude, and as the sand which is by the sea shore innumerable.[13] These all died in faith, not having received the promises, but having seen them afar off, and were persuaded of them, and embraced them, and confessed that they were strangers and pilgrims on the earth.[14] For they that say such things declare plainly that they seek a country.[15] And truly, if they had been mindful of that country from whence they came out, they might have had opportunity to have returned.[16] But now they desire a better country, that is, an heavenly: wherefore God is not ashamed to be called their God: for he hath prepared for them a city.[17] By faith Abraham, when he was tried, offered up Isaac: and he that had received the promises offered up his only begotten son,[18] Of whom it was said, That in Isaac shall thy seed be called:[19] Accounting that God was able to raise him up, even from the dead; from whence also he received him in a figure.[20] By faith Isaac blessed Jacob and Esau concerning things to come.[21] By faith Jacob, when he was a dying, blessed both the sons of Joseph; and worshipped, leaning upon the top of his staff.[22] By faith Joseph, when he died, made mention of the departing of the children of Israel; and gave commandment concerning his bones.[23] By faith Moses, when he was born, was hid three months of his parents, because they saw he was a proper child; and they were not afraid of the king's commandment.[24] By faith Moses, when he was come to years, refused to be called the son of Pharaoh's daughter;[25] Choosing rather to suffer affliction with the people of God, than to enjoy the pleasures of sin for a season;[26] Esteeming the reproach of Christ greater riches than the treasures in Egypt: for he had respect unto the recompence of the reward.[27] By faith he forsook Egypt, not fearing the wrath of the king: for he endured, as seeing him who is invisible.[28] Through faith he kept the passover, and the sprinkling of blood, lest he that destroyed the firstborn should touch them.[29] By faith they passed through the Red sea as by dry land: which the Egyptians assaying to do were drowned.[30] By faith the walls of Jericho fell down, after they were compassed about seven days.[31] By faith the harlot Rahab perished not with them that believed notwhen she had received the spies with peace.[32] And what shall I more say? for the time would fail me to tell of Gedeon, and of Barak, and of Samson, and of Jephthae; of David also, and Samuel, and of the prophets:[33] Who through faith subdued kingdoms, wrought righteousness, obtained promises, stopped the mouths of lions.[34] Quenched the violence of fire, escaped the edge of the sword, out of weakness were made strong, waxed valiant in fight, turned to flight the armies of the aliens.[35] Women received their dead raised to life again: and others were tortured, not accepting deliverance; that they might obtain a better resurrection:[36] And others had trial of cruel mockings and scourgings, yea, moreover of bonds and imprisonment:[37] They were stoned, they were sawn asunder, were tempted, were slain with the sword: they wandered about in sheepskins and goatskins; being destitute, afflicted, tormented;[38] (Of whom the world was not worthy:) they wandered in deserts, and in mountains, and in dens and caves of the earth.[39] And these all, having obtained a good report through faith, received not the promise:[40] God having provided some better thing for us, that they without us should not be made perfect.

12 Wherefore seeing we also are compassed about with so great a cloud of witnesses, let us lay aside every weight, and the sin which doth so easily beset us, and let us run with patience the race that is set before us,[2] Looking unto Jesus the author and finisher of our faith; who for the joy that was set before him endured the cross, despising the shame, and is set down at the right hand of the throne of God.[3] For consider him that endured such contradiction of sinners against himself, lest ye be wearied and faint in your minds.[4] Ye have not yet resisted unto blood, striving against sin.[5] And ye have forgotten the exhortation which speaketh unto you as unto children, My son, despise not thou the chastening of the Lord, nor faint when thou art rebuked of him:[6] For whom the Lord loveth he chasteneth, and scourgeth every son whom he receiveth.[7] If ye endure chastening, God dealeth with you as with sons; for what son is he whom the father chasteneth not?[8] But if ye be without chastisement, whereof all are partakers, then are ye bastards, and not sons.[9] Furthermore we have had fathers of our flesh which corrected us, and we gave them reverence: shall we not much rather be in subjection unto the Father of spirits, and live? For they verily for a few days chastened us after their own pleasure; but he for our profit, that we might be partakers of his holiness.[11] Now no chastening for the present seemeth to be joyous, but grievous: nevertheless afterward it yieldeth the peaceable fruit of righteousness unto them which are exercised thereby.[12] Wherefore lift up the hands which hang down, and the feeble knees;[13] And make straight paths for your feet, lest that which is lame be turned out of the way; but let it rather be healed.[14] Follow peace with all men, and holiness, without which no man shall see the Lord:[15] Looking diligently lest any man fail of the grace of God; lest any root of bitterness springing up trouble you, and thereby many be defiled;[16] Lest there be any fornicator, or profane person, as Esau, who for one morsel of meat sold his birthright.[17] For ye know how that afterward, when he would have inherited the blessing, he was rejected: for he found no place of repentance, though he sought it carefully with tears.[18] For ye are not come unto the mount that might be touched, and that burned with fire, nor unto blackness, and darkness, and tempest,[19] And the sound of a trumpet, and the voice of words; which voice they that heard intreated that the word should not be spoken to them any more:[20] (For they could not endure that which was commanded, And if so much as a beast touch the mountain, it shall be stoned, or thrust through with a dart:[21] And so terrible was the sight, that Moses said, I exceedingly fear and quake:)[22] But ye are come unto mount Sion, and unto the city of the living God, the heavenly Jerusalem, and to an innumerable company of angels,[23] To the general assembly and church of the firstborn, which are written in heaven, and to God the Judge of all, and to the spirits of just men made perfect,[24] And to Jesus the mediator of the new covenant, and to the blood of sprinkling, that speaketh better things than that of Abel.[25] See that ye refuse not him that speaketh. For if they escaped not who refused him that spake on earth, much more shall not we escape, if we turn away from him that speaketh from heaven:[26] Whose voice then shook the earth: but now he hath promised, saying, Yet once more I shake not the earth only, but also heaven.[27] And this word, Yet once more, signifieth the removing of those things that are shaken, as of things that are made, that those things which cannot be shaken may remain.[28] Wherefore we receiving a kingdom which cannot be moved, let us have grace, whereby we may serve God acceptably with reverence and godly fear: [29] For our God is a consuming fire.

Deuteronomy 28 And it shall come to pass, if thou shalt hearken diligently unto the voice of the LORD thy God, to observe and to do all his commandments which I command thee this day, that the LORD thy God will set thee on high above all nations of the earth:² And all these blessings shall come on thee, and overtake thee, if thou shalt hearken unto the voice of the LORD thy God.³ Blessed shalt thou be in the city, and blessed shalt thou be in the field.⁴ Blessed shall be the fruit of thy body, and the fruit of thy ground, and the fruit of thy cattle, the increase of thy kine, and the flocks of thy sheep.⁵ Blessed shall be thy basket and thy store.⁶ Blessed shalt thou be when thou comest in, and blessed shalt thou be when thou goest out.⁷ The LORD shall cause thine enemies that rise up against thee to be smitten before thy face: they shall come out against thee one way, and flee before thee seven ways.⁸ The LORD shall command the blessing upon thee in thy storehouses, and in all that thou settest thine hand unto; and he shall bless thee in the land which the LORD thy God giveth thee.⁹ The LORD shall establish thee an holy people unto himself, as he hath sworn unto thee, if thou shalt keep the commandments of the LORD thy God, and walk in his ways.¹⁰ And all people of the earth shall see that thou art called by the name of the LORD; and they shall be afraid of thee.¹¹ And the LORD shall make thee plenteous in goods, in the fruit of thy body, and in the fruit of thy cattle, and in the fruit of thy ground, in the land which the LORD sware unto thy fathers to give thee.¹² The LORD shall open unto thee his good treasure, the heaven to give the rain unto thy land in his season, and to bless all the work of thine hand: and thou shalt lend unto many nations, and thou shalt not borrow.¹³ And the LORD shall make thee the head, and not the tail; and thou shalt be above only, and thou shalt not be beneath; if that thou hearken unto the commandments of the LORD thy God, which I command thee this day, to observe and to do them:

¹⁴ And thou shalt not go aside from any of the words which I command thee this day, to the right hand, or to the left, to go after other gods to serve them.¹⁵ But it shall come to pass, if thou wilt not hearken unto the voice of the LORD thy God, to observe to do all his commandments and his statutes which I command thee this day; that all these curses shall come upon thee, and overtake thee:¹⁶ Cursed shalt thou be in the city, and cursed shalt thou be in the field.¹⁷ Cursed shall be thy basket and thy store.¹⁸ Cursed shall be the fruit of thy body, and the fruit of thy land, the increase of thy kine, and the flocks of thy sheep.¹⁹ Cursed shalt thou be when thou comest in, and cursed shalt thou be when thou goest out.²⁰ The LORD shall send upon thee cursing, vexation, and rebuke, in all that thou settest thine hand unto for to do, until thou be destroyed, and until thou perish quickly; because of the wickedness of thy doings, whereby thou hast forsaken me.²¹ The LORD shall make the pestilence cleave unto thee, until he have consumed thee from off the land, whither thou goest to possess it.²² The LORD shall smite thee with a consumption, and with a fever, and with an inflammation, and with an extreme burning, and with the sword, and with blasting, and with mildew; and they shall pursue thee until thou perish.²³ And thy heaven that is over thy head shall be brass, and the earth that is under thee shall be iron.²⁴ The LORD shall make the rain of thy land powder and dust: from heaven shall it come down upon thee, until thou be destroyed.²⁵ The LORD shall cause thee to be smitten before thine enemies: thou shalt go out one way against them, and flee seven ways before them: and shalt be removed into all the kingdoms of the earth.²⁶ And thy carcase shall be meat unto all fowls of the air, and unto the beasts of the earth, and no man shall fray them away.²⁷ The LORD will smite thee with the botch of Egypt, and with the emerods, and with the scab, and with the itch, whereof thou canst not be healed.²⁸ The LORD shall smite thee with madness, and blindness, and astonishment of heart:²⁹ And thou shalt grope at noonday, as the blind gropeth in darkness, and thou shalt not prosper in thy ways: and thou shalt be only oppressed and spoiled evermore, and no man shall save thee.³⁰ Thou shalt betroth a wife, and another man shall lie with her: thou shalt build an house, and thou shalt not dwell therein: thou shalt

plant a vineyard, and shalt not gather the grapes thereof.[31] Thine ox shall be slain before thine eyes, and thou shalt not eat thereof: thine ass shall be violently taken away from before thy face, and shall not be restored to thee: thy sheep shall be given unto thine enemies, and thou shalt have none to rescue them.[32] Thy sons and thy daughters shall be given unto another people, and thine eyes shall look, and fail with longing for them all the day long; and there shall be no might in thine hand.[33] The fruit of thy land, and all thy labours, shall a nation which thou knowest not eat up; and thou shalt be only oppressed and crushed alway:[34] So that thou shalt be mad for the sight of thine eyes which thou shalt see.[35] The LORD shall smite thee in the knees, and in the legs, with a sore botch that cannot be healed, from the sole of thy foot unto the top of thy head.[36] The LORD shall bring thee, and thy king which thou shalt set over thee, unto a nation which neither thou nor thy fathers have known; and there shalt thou serve other gods, wood and stone.[37] And thou shalt become an astonishment, a proverb, and a byword, among all nations whither The LORD shall lead thee.[38] Thou shalt carry much seed out into the field, and shalt gather but little in; for the locust shall consume it.[39] Thou shalt plant vineyards, and dress them, but shalt neither drink of the wine, nor gather the grapes; for the worms shall eat them.[40] Thou shalt have olive trees throughout all thy coasts, but thou shalt not anoint thyself with the oil; for thine olive shall cast his fruit.[41] Thou shalt beget sons and daughters, but thou shalt not enjoy them for they shall go into captivity.[42] All thy trees and fruit of thy land shall the locust consume.[43] The stranger that is within thee shall get up above thee very high; and thou shalt come down very low.[44] He shall lend to thee, and thou shalt not lend to him: he shall be the head, and thou shalt be the tail.[45] Moreover all these curses shall come upon thee, and shall pursue thee, and overtake thee, till thou be destroyed; because thou hearkenedst not unto the voice of the LORD thy God, to keep his commandments and his statutes which he commanded thee:[46] And they shall be upon thee for a sign and for a wonder, and upon thy seed forever.[47] Because thou servedst not the LORD thy God with joyfulness, and with gladness of heart, for the abundance of all things;[48] Therefore shalt thou serve thine enemies which the LORD shall send against thee, in hunger, and in thirst, and in nakedness, and in want of all things: and he shall put a yoke of iron upon thy neck, until he have destroyed thee.[49] The LORD shall bring a nation against thee from far, from the end of the earth, as swift as the eagle flieth; a nation whose tongue thou shalt not understand;[50] A nation of fierce countenance, which shall not regard the person of the old, nor shew favour to the young:[51] And he shall eat the fruit of thy cattle, and the fruit of thy land, until thou be destroyed: which also shall not leave thee either corn, wine, or oil, or the increase of thy kine, or flocks of thy sheep, until he have destroyed thee.[52] And he shall besiege thee in all thy gates, until thy high and fenced walls come down, wherein thou trustedst, throughout all thy land: and he shall besiege thee in all thy gates throughout all thy land, which the LORD thy God hath given thee.[53] And thou shalt eat the fruit of thine own body, the flesh of thy sons and of thy daughters, which the LORD thy God hath given thee, in the siege, and in the straitness, wherewith thine enemies shall distress thee:[54] So that the man that is tender among you, and very delicate, his eye shall be evil toward his brother,and toward the wife of his bosom, and toward the remnant of his children which he shall leave:[55] So that he will not give to any of them of the flesh of his children whom he shall eat: because he hath nothing left him in the siege, and in the straitness, wherewith thine enemies shall distress thee in all thy gates.[56] The tender and delicate woman among you, which would not adventure to set the sole of her foot upon the ground for delicateness and tenderness, her eye shall be evil toward the husband of her bosom, and toward her son, and toward her daughter,[57] And toward her young one that cometh out from between her feet, and toward her children which she shall bear: for she shall eat them for want of all things secretly in the siege and straitness, wherewith thine enemy shall distress thee in thy gates.[58] If thou wilt not observe to do all the words of this law that are written in this book, that thou mayest fear this glorious and fearful name, THE LORD THY GOD;[59] Then the LORD will make thy plagues wonderful, and the plagues of thy seed, even great plagues, and of long continuance, and sore sicknesses, and of long continuance.[60] Moreover he will bring upon thee all the diseases of Egypt, which thou wast afraid of; and they shall cleave unto thee.⁶¹ Also every sickness, and every plague, which is not written in the book of this law, them will theLORD bring upon thee, until thou be destroyed.⁶² And ye shall be left few in number, whereas ye were as the stars of heaven for multitude; because thou wouldest not obey the voice of the LORD thy God.⁶³ And it shall come to pass, that as the LORD rejoiced over you to do you good, and to multiply you; so the LORD will rejoice over you to destroy you, and to bring you to nought; and ye shall be plucked from off the land whither thou goest to possess it.⁶⁴ And the LORD shall scatter thee among all people, from the one end of the earth even unto the other; and there thou shalt serve other gods, which neither thou nor thy fathers have known, even wood and stone.⁶⁵ And among these nations shalt thou find no ease, neither shall the sole of thy foot have rest: but the LORD shall give thee there a trembling heart, and failing of eyes, and sorrow of mind:⁶⁶ And thy life shall hang in doubt before thee; and thou shalt fear day and night, and shalt have none assurance of thy life:⁶⁷ In the morning thou shalt say, Would God it were even! and at even thou shalt say, Would God it were morning! for the fear of thine heart wherewith thou shalt fear, and for the sight of thine eyes which thou shalt see.⁶⁸ And the LORD shall bring thee into Egypt again with ships, by the way whereof I spake unto thee, Thou shalt see it no more again: and there ye shall be sold unto your enemies for bondmen and bondwomen, and no man shall buy you.

29 These are the words of the covenant, which the LORD commanded Moses to make with the children of Israel in the land of Moab, beside the covenant which he made with them in Horeb.² And Moses called unto all Israel, and said unto them, Ye have seen all that the LORD did before your eyes in the land of Egypt unto Pharaoh, and unto all his servants, and unto all his land;³ The great temptations which thine eyes have seen, the signs, and those great miracles:⁴ Yet the LORD hath not given you an heart to perceive, and eyes to see, and ears to hear, unto this day.⁵ And I have led you forty years in the wilderness: your clothes are not waxen old upon you, and thy shoe is not waxen old upon thy foot.⁶ Ye have not eaten bread, neither have ye drunk wine or strong drink: that ye might know that I am the LORD your God.⁷ And when ye

came unto this place, Sihon the king of Heshbon, and Og the king of Bashan, came outagainst us unto battle, and we smote them:[8] And we took their land, and gave it for an inheritance unto the Reubenites, and to the Gadites, and to the half tribe of Manasseh.[9] Keep therefore the words of this covenant, and do them, that ye may prosper in all that ye do.[10] Ye stand this day all of you before the LORD your God; your captains of your tribes, your elders, and your officers, with all the men of Israel,[11] Your little ones, your wives, and thy stranger that is in thy camp, from the hewer of thy wood unto the drawer of thy water:[12] That thou shouldest enter into covenant with the LORD thy God, and into his oath, which the LORDthy God maketh with thee this day:[13] That he may establish thee today for a people unto himself, and that he may be unto thee a God, as the hath said unto thee, and as he hath sworn unto thy fathers, to Abraham, to Isaac, and to Jacob.[14] Neither with you only do I make this covenant and this oath;[15] But with him that standeth here with us this day before the LORD our God, and also with him that is not here with us this day:[16] (For ye know how we have dwelt in the land of Egypt; and how we came through the nations which ye passed by;[17] And ye have seen their abominations, and their idols, wood and stone, silver and gold, which were among them:)[18] Lest there should be among you man, or woman, or family, or tribe, whose heart turneth away this day from the LORD our God, to go and serve the gods of these nations; lest there should be among you a root that beareth gall and wormwood;[19] And it come to pass, when he heareth the words of this curse, that he bless himself in his heart, saying, I shall have peace, though I walk in the imagination of mine heart, to add drunkenness to thirst:[20] The LORD will not spare him, but then the anger of the LORD and his jealousy shall smoke against that man, and all the curses that are written in this book shall lie upon him, and the LORD shall blot out his name from under heaven.[21] And the LORD shall separate him unto evil out of all the tribes of Israel according to all the curses of the covenant that are written in this book of the law:[22] So that the generation to come of your children that shall rise up after you, and the stranger that shall come from a far land, shall say, when they see the plagues of that land, and the sicknesses which the LORD hath laid upon it;[23] And that the whole land thereof is brimstone, and salt, and burning, that it is not sown, nor beareth, nor any grass groweth therein, like the overthrow of Sodom, an Gomorrah, Admah, and Zeboim, which the LORD overthrew in his anger, and in his wrath:[24] Even all nations shall say, Wherefore hath the LORD done thus unto this land? what meaneth the heat of this great anger?[25] Then men shall say, Because they have forsaken the covenant of the LORD God of their fathers, which he made with them when he brought them forth out of the land of Egypt:[26] For they went and served other gods, and worshipped them, gods whom they knew not, and whom he had not given unto them:[27] And the anger of the LORD was kindled against this land, to bring upon it all the curses that are written in this book:[28] And the LORD rooted them out of their land in anger, and in wrath, and in great indignation, and cast them into another land, as it is this day.[29] The secret things belong unto the LORD our God: but those things which are revealed belong unto us and to our children forever, that we may do all the words of this law.

30 And it shall come to pass, when all these things are come upon thee, the blessing and the curse, which I have set before thee, and thou shalt call them to mind among all the nations, whither the LORD thy God hath driven thee,[2] And shalt return unto the LORD thy God, and shalt obey his voice according to all that I command thee this day, thou and thy children, with all thine heart, and with all thy soul;[3] That then the LORD thy God will turn thy captivity, and have compassion upon thee, and will return and gather thee from all the nations, whither the LORD thy God hath scattered thee.[4] If any of thine be driven out unto the outmost parts of heaven, from thence will the LORD thy God gather thee, and from thence will he fetch thee:[5] And the LORD thy God will bring thee into the land which thy fathers possessed, and thou shalt possess it; and he will do thee good, and multiply thee above thy fathers.[6] And the LORD thy God will circumcise thine heart, and the heart of thy seed, to love the LORD thy God with all thine heart, and with all thy soul, that thou mayest live.[7] And the LORD thy God will put all these curses upon thine enemies, and on them that hate thee, which persecuted thee.[8] And thou shalt return and obey the voice of the LORD, and do all his commandments which I command thee this day.[9] And the LORD thy God will make thee plenteous in every work of thine hand, in the fruit of thy body, and in the fruit of thy cattle, and in the fruit of thy land, for good: for the LORD will again rejoice over thee for good, as he rejoiced over thy fathers:[10] If thou shalt hearken unto the voice of the LORD thy God, to keep his commandments and his statutes which are written in this book of the law, and if thou turn unto the LORD thy God with all thine heart, and with all thy soul.[11] For this commandment which I command thee this day, it is not hidden from thee, neither is it far off.[12] It is not in heaven, that thou shouldest say, Who shall go up for

us to heaven, and bring it unto us, that we may hear it, and do it?[13] Neither is it beyond the sea, that thou shouldest say, Who shall go over the sea for us, and bring it unto us, that we may hear it, and do it?[14] But the word is very nigh unto thee, in thy mouth, and in thy heart, that thou mayest do it.[15] See, I have set before thee this day life and good, and death and evil;[16] In that I command thee this day to love the LORD thy God, to walk in his ways, and to keep his commandments and his statutes and his judgments, that thou mayest live and multiply: and the LORD thy God shall bless thee in the land whither thou goest to possess it.[17] But if thine heart turn away, so that thou wilt not hear, but shalt be drawn away, and worship other gods, and serve them;[18] I denounce unto you this day, that ye shall surely perish, and that ye shall not prolong your days upon the land, whither thou passest over Jordan to go to possess it.[19] I call heaven and earth to record this day against you, that I have set before you life and death, blessing and cursing: therefore choose life, that both thou and thy seed may live:[20] That thou mayest love the LORD thy God, and that thou mayest obey his voice, and that thou mayest cleave unto him: for he is thy life, and the length of thy days: that thou mayest dwell in the land which the LORD sware unto thy fathers, to Abraham, to Isaac, and to Jacob, to give them

31 And Moses went and spake these words unto all Israel.[2] And he said unto them, I am an hundred and twenty years old this day; I can no more go out and come in: also the LORD hath said unto me, Thou shalt not go over this Jordan.[3] The LORD thy God, he will go over before thee, and he will destroy these nations from before thee, and thou shalt possess them: and Joshua, he shall go over before thee, as the LORD hath said.[4] And the LORD shall do unto them as he did to Sihon and to Og, kings of the Amorites, and unto the land of them, whom he destroyed.[5] And the LORD shall give them up before your face, that ye may do unto them according unto all the commandments which I have commanded you.[6] Be strong and of a good courage, fear not, nor be afraid of them: for the LORD thy God, he it is that doth go with thee; he will not fail thee, nor forsake thee.[7] And Moses called unto Joshua, and said unto him in the sight of all Israel, Be strong and of a good courage: for thou must go with this people unto the land which the LORD hath sworn unto their fathers to give them; and thou shalt cause them to inherit it.[8] And the LORD, he it is that doth go before thee; he will be with thee, he will not fail thee, neither forsake thee: fear not, neither be dismayed.[9] And Moses wrote this law, and delivered it unto the priests

the sons of Levi, which bare the ark of the covenant of the LORD, and unto all the elders of Israel.¹⁰ And Moses commanded them, saying, At the end of every seven years, in the solemnity of the year of release, in the feast of tabernacles,¹¹ When all Israel is come to appear before the LORD thy God in the place which he shall choose, thou shalt read this law before all Israel in their hearing.¹² Gather the people together, men and women, and children, and thy stranger that is within thy gates, that they may hear, and that they may learn, and fear the LORD your God, and observe to do all thewords of this law:¹³ And that their children, which have not known anything, may hear, and learn to fear the LORD your God, as long as ye live in the land whither ye go over Jordan to possess it.¹⁴ And the LORD said unto Moses, Behold, thy days approach that thou must die: call Joshua, and present yourselves in the tabernacle of the congregation, that I may give him a charge. And Moses and Joshua went, and presented themselves in the tabernacle of the congregation.¹⁵ And the LORD appeared in the tabernacle in a pillar of a cloud: and the pillar of the cloud stood over the door of the tabernacle.¹⁶ And the LORD said unto Moses, Behold, thou shalt sleep with thy fathers; and this people will rise up, and go a whoring after the gods of the strangers of the land, whither they go to be among them, and will forsake me, and break my covenant which I have made with them.¹⁷ Then my anger shall be kindled against them in that day, and I will forsake them, and I will hide my face from them, and they shall be devoured, and many evils and troubles shall befall them; so that they will say in that day, Are not these evils come upon us, because our God is not among us?¹⁸ And I will surely hide my face in that day for all the evils which they shall have wrought, in that they are turned unto other gods.¹⁹ Now therefore write ye this song for you, and teach it the children of Israel: put it in their mouths, that this song may be a witness for me against the children of Israel.²⁰ For when I shall have brought them into the land which I sware unto their fathers, that floweth with milk and honey; and they shall have eaten and filled themselves, and waxen fat; then will they turn unto other gods, and serve them, and provoke me, and break my covenant.²¹ And it shall come to pass, when many evils and troubles are befallen them, that this song shall testify against them as a witness; for it shall not be forgotten out of the mouths of their seed: for I know their imagination which they go about, even now, before I have brought them into the land which I sware.²² Moses therefore wrote this song the same day, and taught it the children of Israel.²³ And he gave Joshua the son of Nun a charge, and said, Be strong and of a good courage: for thou shalt bring the children of Israel into the land which I sware unto them: and I will be with thee.[24] And it came to pass, when Moses had made an end of writing the words of this law in a book, until they were finished,[25] That Moses commanded the Levites, which bare the ark of the covenant of the LORD, saying,[26] Take this book of the law, and put it in the side of the ark of the covenant of the LORD your God, that it may be there for a witness against thee.[27] For I know thy rebellion, and thy stiff neck: behold, while I am yet alive with you this day, ye have been rebellious against the LORD; and how much more after my death?[28] Gather unto me all the elders of your tribes, and your officers, that I may speak these words in their ears, and call heaven and earth to record against them.[29] For I know that after my death ye will utterly corrupt yourselves, and turn aside from the way which I have commanded you; and evil will befall you in the latter days; because ye will do evil in the sight of the LORD, to provoke him to anger through the work of your hands.[30] And Moses spake in the ears of all the congregation of Israel the words of this song, until they were ended.

32 Give ear, O ye heavens, and I will speak; and hear, O earth, the words of my mouth.[2] My doctrine shall drop as the rain, my speech shall distil as the dew, as the small rain upon the tender herb, and as the showers upon the grass:[3] Because I will publish the name of the LORD: ascribe ye greatness unto our God.[4] He is the Rock, his work is perfect: for all his ways are judgment: a God of truth and without iniquity, just and right is he.[5] They have corrupted themselves, their spot is not the spot of his children: they are a perverse and crooked generation.[6] Do ye thus requite the LORD, O foolish people and unwise? is not he thy father that hath bought thee? hath he not made thee, and established thee?[7] Remember the days of old, consider the years of many generations: ask thy father, and he will shew thee; thy elders, and they will tell thee.[8] When the Most High divided to the nations their inheritance, when he separated the sons of Adam, he set the bounds of the people according to the number of the children of Israel.[9] For the LORD's portion is his people; Jacob is the lot of his inheritance.[10] He found him in a desert land, and in the waste howling wilderness; he led him about, he instructed him, he kept him as the apple of his eye.[11] As an eagle stirreth up her nest, fluttereth over her young, spreadeth abroad her wings, taketh them, beareth them on her wings:[12] So the LORD alone did lead him, and there was no strange god with

him.[13] He made him ride on the high places of the earth, that he might eat the increase of the fields; and he made him to suck honey out of the rock, and oil out of the flinty rock;[14] Butter of kine, and milk of sheep, with fat of lambs, and rams of the breed of Bashan, and goats, with the fat of kidneys of wheat; and thou didst drink the pure blood of the grape.[15] But Jeshurun waxed fat, and kicked: thou art waxen fat, thou art grown thick, thou art covered with fatness; then he forsook God which made him, and lightly esteemed the Rock of his salvation.[16] They provoked him to jealousy with strange gods, with abominations provoked they him to anger.[17] They sacrificed unto devils, not to God; to gods whom they knew not, to new gods that came newly up, whom your fathers feared not.[18] Of the Rock that begat thee thou art unmindful, and hast forgotten God that formed thee.[19] And when the LORD saw it, he abhorred them, because of the provoking of his sons, and of his daughters.[20] And he said, I will hide my face from them, I will see what their end shall be: for they are a very froward generation, children in whom is no faith.[21] They have moved me to jealousy with that which is not God; they have provoked me to anger with their vanities: and I will move them to jealousy with those which are not a people; I will provoke them to anger with a foolish nation.[22] For a fire is kindled in mine anger, and shall burn unto the lowest hell, and shall consume the earth with her increase, and set on fire the foundations of the mountains.[23] I will heap mischiefs upon them; I will spend mine arrows upon them.[24] They shall be burnt with hunger, and devoured with burning heat, and with bitter destruction: I will also send the teeth of beasts upon them, with the poison of serpents of the dust.[25] The sword without, and terror within, shall destroy both the young man and the virgin, the suckling also with the man of gray hairs.[26] I said, I would scatter them into corners, I would make the remembrance of them to cease from among men:[27] Were it not that I feared the wrath of the enemy, lest their adversaries should behave themselves strangely, and lest they should say, Our hand is high, and the LORD hath not done all this.[28] For they are a nation void of counsel, neither is there any understanding in them.[29] O that they were wise, that they understood this, that they would consider their latter end![30] How should one chase a thousand, and two put ten thousand to flight, except their Rock had sold them, and the LORD had shut them up?[31] For their rock is not as our Rock, even our enemies themselves being judges.[32] For their vine is of the vine of Sodom, and of the fields of Gomorrah: their grapes are grapes of gall, their clusters are bitter:[33] Their wine is the poison of dragons, and the cruel venom of asps.[34] Is not this laid up in store with me, and sealed up among my treasures?[35] To me belongeth vengeance and recompence; their foot shall slide in due time: for the day of their calamity is at hand, and the things that shall come upon them make haste.[36] For the LORD shall judge his people, and repent himself for his servants, when he seeth that their power is gone, and there is none shut up, or left.[37] And he shall say, Where are their gods, their rock in whom they trusted,[38] Which did eat the fat of their sacrifices, and drank the wine of their drink offerings? let them rise up and help you, and be your protection.[39] See now that I, even I, am he, and there is no god with me: I kill, and I make alive; I wound, and I heal: neither is there any that can deliver out of my hand.[40] For I lift up my hand to heaven, and say, I live forever.[41] If I whet my glittering sword, and mine hand take hold on judgment; I will render vengeance to mine enemies, and will reward them that hate me.[42] I will make mine arrows drunk with blood, and my sword shall devour flesh; and that with the blood of the slain and of the captives, from the beginning of revenges upon the enemy.[43] Rejoice, O ye nations, with his people: for he will avenge the blood of his servants, and will render vengeance to his adversaries, and will be merciful unto his land, and to his people.[44] And Moses came and spake all the words of this song in the ears of the people, he, and Hoshea the son of Nun.[45] And Moses made an end of speaking all these words to all Israel:[46] And he said unto them, Set your hearts unto all the words which I testify among you this day, which You shall command your children to observe to do, all the words of this law.[47] For it is not a vain thing for you; because it is your life: and through this thing ye shall prolong your days in the land, whither ye go over Jordan to possess it.[48] And the LORD spake unto Moses that selfsame day, saying,[49] Get thee up into this mountain Abarim, unto mount Nebo, which is in the land of Moab, that is over against Jericho; and behold the land of Canaan, which I give unto the children of Israel for a possession:[50] And die in the mount whither thou goest up, and be gathered unto thy people; as Aaron thy brother died in mount Hor, and was gathered unto his people:[51] Because ye trespassed against me among the children of Israel at the waters of MeribahKadesh, in the wilderness of Zin; because ye sanctified me not in the midst of the children of Israel.[52] Yet thou shalt see the land before thee; but thou shalt not go thither unto the land which I give the children of Israel.

Doubt is not an obstacle, faith is. Seeing through the unknown destroys fear. Belief is faith, the guided missile that hits the target to a victorious life. Faith can be misplaced. Faith can be corrupted, destroyed, and manipulated. So to destroy doubt is to explore faith. Your obstacle may be a simply change of mind into the faith of believing what others cannot see, refuse to see, or for have given up on looking. It's OK. It is your choice to remain in the unscientific ignorance and insubordination of doubt.

CHAPTER 6

That is ridiculous!

Skepticism is the tool solely designed to attack leadership. If it wasn't for skepticism, no dreams would have ever been shattered. Can you imagine having the freedom to imagine, to not be condemned for a simple expression like, "what if...?" Skepticism has destroyed remedies. Skepticism has held back the cure of cancer. Skepticism has delayed progress on every level in every industry for every government and every resolve for eons. Skepticism is the number one cause of every neglected attempt for success. Skepticism is more than just criticism. Skepticism is a wet blanket on every hope kindled. To destroy hope is the neutron bomb in every demons arsenal. They want you, but they do not want you hopeful, happy, or historical! Skepticism is the ultimate history rewrite. All the expressions of "the-what-could-have-been" over time are the direct result of skeptical communication, skeptical attitudes, or skeptical looks.

Ezekiel 2:6 And thou, son of man, be not afraid of them, neither be afraid of their words, though briers and thorns be with thee, and thou does well among scorpions: be not afraid of their words, nor be dismayed at their looks, though they be a rebellious house.

In the last few weeks, I have experienced every form of skepticism, from every level of relationship in my life. I was speaking to a family member about my decision to run for U.S. Senate, not only could I feel the look on their face, but the words that followed the silence were stifling. I then received several messages on all the reasons why I could not do what I was about to do. Then a team mate that was helping me sent an email to someone, it was not intended for my eyes, but accidentally got sent to my email? It was almost completely disabling. In fact, it robbed me of several hours of sleep, and with the morning sun I was all but defeated from even getting started. Oddly enough, this was not sent with the intentions I had thought, but I was already being influenced by skeptics that it made me blinded to the sincerity of others. I was turning into that commercial that starts off with a friendly, "Good Morning".

Not knowing that that early that day this poor soul experienced a misread of someone else's intentions and was harboring the bitterness of hurt and shattered dreams. So in response to the "Good Morning!", the person bites back..."Yeah, what's good about it?"

This starts a series of interactions that eventually sends the entire high rise into riot of throwing their chairs and desks out the windows. This is the ends of skepticism.

Then the Facebook messages started to come! I received from the naysayers, the opposites, the unfriendly, the unkind, the deviate, and the outright discouragers. One even asked of me," Who do you think you are running for political office with that kind of thinking?" My intent to run for office was to do what others have failed at doing, represent me! I don't know, I just had this random thought that because I was an American concerned citizen and that the decisions being made on my behalf did not represent my concerns or that as different as my thought process may be, it was my freedom to speak? I didn't say anyone had to listen? But at least I decide to do something about what I believe, rather than complain about it every day! M.C. Hammer said it best, "we got to pray just to make it today"! Or how J.LO put it, "You can hard or you can home"! For all the criticism, Eminem said it the best, "You got to lose yourself in the moment"! I actually do not believe any of these intended to try to discourage me. It may have been their sincere love for me that didn't want me to have to expose myself to the cruelty of humankind or myself and family to the worse of what is yet to come, the manipulative suicide promoting media. If we can make drama out of someone's life, let us do what we can do to destroy someone's dreams. The traditional media on every level is the giant of skepticism.

Whether it is condescension, ridicule, or purposeful discouragement, the media is the greatest of the promoters of "EEYORE MENTALITY". Let's put a gray cloud over the day and see if people will jump off of buildings? Let's insight a riot! Now this is my skepticism...see how easily we are influenced. The breeding of hatred, division, variance, and malice is seeded by skepticism. An ancient term for this is, "Froward". "Froward", is the expression of upside down.

It is the physical representation of the frown of discouragement, sadness, despair, depravity, emptiness, hopelessness. I really cannot imagine anyone having these goals in their life? I have been told it takes many times more muscles to frown than to smile. To smile is the relaxing of facial muscle; the stress free life of smile contentment. If there is one thing I get accused of more than anything else and that is that I smile all the time! If I am not smiling, something is seriously wrong. I have a hard time smiling while my daughter is vomiting from chemo poisoning. When I got the call my mom died just after I left her, I wasn't smiling. When I was feeding my father breakfast and he died with a spoonful of LIFE cereal at his mouth, I didn't smile right away. I now smile at these things. I smile that my mom is in heaven and would never ask her to sacrifice the joys of heaven for the times I need her here. I smile in the room where we cared for my dad. Where I sit even now as I write. We call this now the heaven room. For that brief fragment of time, my hand was inside the portals of heaven. LIFE cereal, come on folks, now that's either funny; or absolute destiny! Maybe it is insanity, but my wife and I sometimes can't help but laugh, as we are out with buckets scrubbing furniture, floors, carpets, and clothes of something to the like of "ecto-plasma" out of Ghost Buster's? Exhausted, frantic, and just shy of ridiculous, we fall against each other, in what else can we do smirk and chuckle because we are not defeated! We were told that 70% of marriages fall apart through this. I completely understand how and why. The very reason for starting the Selah Says Society was to help other families through the overwhelming skepticisms of pediatric protocol, pharmaceutical prosperities, medicinal minutiae, oncological overload, hospital harassment, and financial frantic for the fornication of freedoms frequently forgotten for families everywhere. I would like to explain or expound on that last statement.

As we set out donations jars for Selah Says Society, a regular comment may be something like this, "Wow, I wish I could set jars and have others put money it and not have to work for a living?" Oh really?

You want to give up your regular income to go sleepless for days at a time while your greatest treasure is managed through death, fevers, convulsions, nausea, diarrhea, and hellacious side effects? One time during the process we gave up putting diapers on our daughter after using 40 in a day. It was easier to just through sheets away! Is that what you want for your skeptical self? Or be questioned by others, I thought your child was in remission? Remission does not mean the stopping of protocol. This is a minimum 2 ½ year event for females and 3 year minimum for boys. This is only if everything goes well! Then there is a lifelong hold your breath that nothing recurs. That every time your child gets a fever, you expect to be hospitalized due to a compromised immune system. Or the long term effect that could damage other organs, cognitive abilities, and eye site. Then there is the overall anxiety of the family. The concerns of other siblings, being robbed of their lives, their family time, and their loss of freedoms are real. Mom and Dad intimate time is what is left over. Which is usually nothing? Exhausted, worn, frazzled, and emptied you forge on. If everyone in the United States gave $20 this year, we might be able to manage through investment scruples the relief of income to the families experiencing pediatric cancer for a lifetime. No one considers the cost of gas, time, insurance, and thieving, costs of jars, labels, banking, decorations, income replacement, and renovation expenses; clean up, non-covered expenses, support therapy, home alterations, situational rising energy costs, travel expenses, and other life managements when someone drops three cents into a donation jar. Or their old toothpicks, gum wrappers, trash, or worse? So you go by to pick up a dollar after a week? Even if you were able to regularly collect $500 a week, how many families could you seriously help? But this is skepticism talking now!

It was skepticism that shed the first human blood. Cain being skeptical of Abel's gift and favor verses his own sacrifices. If Cain would have given what God asked, he too would have experienced the manifold blessings of obedience! It was skepticism that nearly eliminated humankind. What in the world is "rain" Noah?

It was skepticism that caused millions to wander. Moses you surely brought us out here to starve and thirst!

It is skepticism that brings the judgment of God. But skeptics are not our obstacle...Leadership is.

There are multiple forms of psychological leadership methods; Strong arm; Group concepts; Distribution of authority; Micromanagement; and Theocratic. The bottom line is that someone has to be accountable and responsible for the direction and decisions. This is Leadership.

Truth is something that never has to be shied away from, coward, or to fear. In fact, truth is sword forward charge! There are plenty of people you can find who like to boss others around, but very few that stand in the responsibility of truth. We call this integrity! We call this tenacity! We call this leadership!

Jeremiah 30:10 Therefore fear thou not, O my servant Jacob, saith the lord; neither be dismayed, O Israel: for, lo, I will save thee from afar, and thy seed from the land of their captivity; and Jacob shall return, and shall be in rest, and be quiet, and none shall make him afraid.

Jeremiah 10:2 Thus saith the Lord, Learn not the way of the heathen, and be dismayed at the signs of heaven, for the heathen are dismayed at them.

Jeremiah 1:17 Thou therefore gird up thy loins, and arise, and speak unto them all that I command thee: be not dismayed at their faces, lest I confound thee before them.

Isaiah 41:10 Fear thou not; I am with thee: be not dismayed; for I am thy God: I will strengthen thee; yea, I will help thee; yea, I will uphold thee with the right hand of my righteousness.

1 Chronicles 28:20 And David said to Solomon his son, Be strong and of a good courage, and do it: fear not, nor be dismayed: for the Lord God, even my God, will be with thee; he will not fail thee, nor forsake thee, until thou hast finished all the work for the services of the house of the Lord.

Joshua 1:9 Have not I commanded thee? Be strong and of a good courage; be not afraid, neither be thou dismayed: for the Lord thy God is with whithersoever thou goest.

Deuteronomy 31:8 And the lord, he it is that doth go before thee; he will be with thee, he will not fail thee, neither forsake thee: fear not, neither be dismayed.

Leadership is simply seeing a target and managing the road map knowing that everyone involved doesn't have the privilege to see the whole picture or final destination. So the need for communication becomes the key to leadership. That vision, that target, that reminder must be communicated in a way with no variance, no weak links...we call this discipline. Without truth we have no destination or direction. Without faith we have no drive. Without leadership we have no discipleship.

Skepticism is sent for the sole purpose of disrupting discipline, action, management, and leadership.

Proverbs 4:23-25 Keep your heart with all diligence; for out of it are the issues of life. Put away from you a forward (upside down) mouth, and perverse lips put far from you. Let your eyes look right on(straight forward), and let your eyelids look straight before you.

Proverbs 11;20 They that are of a forward heart are abomination to the Lord.

Matthew 15:16 And Jesus said, Are you also without understanding? Do you yet understand, that whatsoever enters in at the mouth goes into your belly and is cast out into the draught ('flushed like a turd') But those things which proceed out of your mouth come from the heart; and they defile us. For out of the heart proceed evil thoughts, murders, adulteries, fornications, thefts, false witness, blasphemies; these are the things that defile you!

Surgery required... "Opthorectomology". Something has gotten in the way of our ability to see truth, our third eye is blind, it is time for a serious cleanse when your vision is skewed by the waste that scholars, politicians, doctors, lawyers, sales people, and false spiritual leaders have clogged your processing with cover up, deceit, lies, dishonesty, hatred, pride, greed, and failed leadership!

So, say no to the skeptic, they are not leaders. Say yes to truth, yes to passion, yes to desire, yes to the dreams and visions you have seen of yourself, despite yourself and despite what others do not see, cannot see, or will not see. Do not let the scars of other's failures deter you from what can be. You are LEAD. You are FORWARD. You are the CHARGE. You are the CATALYST for which the world is waiting.

You are YOU! BE! BEHOLD! BECOME BETTER! BE OUTRAGEOUS! BE HAPPY! BEAUTIFUL in TRUTH! OBSTACLE FREE! GO! DO! YEAH!

Chapter 7

This is the Conclusion of the Matter

What if you could see, what you don't?

Your entire life is spent overcoming obstacles; obstacles of success, health, happiness, and dreams coming true. Whether you understand this or not there is an opposing force? You have an adversary!

You have someone that continually tries to create diversions to your peace. Is not peace what we really all want? We are sold the lie of prosperity, success, glory, fame, fashion, and genius. A week rarely passes that we do not hear about people around this terrestrial who apparently have what we were all sold to pursue in shipwreck, suicide, overdose, rehab, broken, worn, and even imprisonment. The freedoms they were lied to about have robbed all that for which life is worth living. They could not see that the temporal is empty. The temporal gets stolen. The temporal gets broken. The temporal leaves us, forsakes us, and misdirects us. There is so much more to see in this life, through this mind, outside of these eyes, in the eternals.

The wings of the hummingbird lose their curiosity and beauty in the slowed down version. It is in the reality of what we do not see that their greatest beauty thrives. I imagine the angelic, the spiritual in much the same way, too fast for our limited shutter speed. So let us experience this reality in the fullness of design. The Psalmist writes; open thou mine eyes, that I may behold wondrous things out of thy law , and again writes, for thou hast been a shelter for me, and a strong tower from the enemy, but we cannot see for what we are looking. A brother of Jesus of Nazareth writes: Keep yourselves in the love of God, looking for the mercy of our Lord Jesus Christ unto eternal life. If you are looking in the mirror and you see you...you have been duped.

...For behold the Kingdom of God is within you!

Why do we go to funerals to see the dead, because they are not there!

On that triumphant day that so many celebrate and so often forget, it was said..."Why seek ye the living among the dead?"

We choose to listen to those who have no hope?

1 Thessalonians 4:13 But I would not have you ignorant, brethren, concerning them which are asleep, that ye sorrow not, even as others which have no hope. I challenge you, as I challenge myself, to go reread Romans Eight and be encouraged, edified, reconstructed, reproved, restored, and resurrected.

John 12:40 He hath blinded their eyes, and hardened their heart; that they should not see with their eyes, nor understand with their heart, and be converted, and I (God) should heal them.

2 Kings 6:17 And Elisha prayed, and said, Lord, I pray thee, open his eyes, that he may see. And the Lord opened the eyes of the young man; and he saw: and, behold, the mountain was full of horses and chariots of fire about Elisha.

The amazement of this story is that the horses were already there along with the chariots. So what was it that the young man had blocking his eyes? Because, it also declares his eyes were opened? Elisha already saw them! His confidence was secure! His hope lodged within what others could not see! The skepticism, fears, doubts, lack of desire, the hindrances from getting over the true obstacles, blocked the truth that other things take place on this planet, inside selective worlds, spinning on this terrestrial ball that defy physical law, human reasoning, and harboring excuses that limit life that could be lived.

Now faith is the substance of things hoped for, the evidence of things not seen! Hebrews 12:1

1. Start looking for what others do not
2. Start seeking truth
3. Start seeing something bigger then you in the mirror
4. Ask God to open your eyes
5. Start living outside of you what actually is in you
6. Start seeing yourself as God sees you...Forgiven
7. Don't get blinded by the enemies of truth

JOHN 12 Then Jesus six days before the passover came to Bethany, where Lazarus was, which had been dead, whom he raised from the dead.[2] There they made him a supper; and Martha served: but Lazarus was one of them that sat at the table with him.[3] Then took Mary a pound of ointment of spikenard, very costly, and anointed the feet of Jesus, and wiped his feet with her hair: and the house was filled with the odour the ointment.[4] Then saith one of his disciples, Judas Iscariot, Simon's son, which should betray him,[5] Why was not this ointment sold for three hundred pence, and given to the poor?[6] This he said, not that he cared for the poor; but because he was a thief, and had the bag, and bare what was put therein.[7] Then said Jesus, Let her alone: against the day of my burying hath she kept this.[8] For the poor always ye have with you; but me ye have not always.[9] Much people of the Jews therefore knew that he was there: and they came not for Jesus' sake only, but that they might see Lazarus also, whom he had raised from the dead.[10] But the chief priests consulted that they might put Lazarus also to death;[11] Because that by reason of him many of the Jews went away, and believed on Jesus.[12] On the next day much people that were come to the feast, when they heard that Jesus was coming to Jerusalem,[13] Took branches of palm trees, and went forth to meet him, and cried, Hosanna: Blessed is the King of Israel that cometh in the name of the Lord.[14] And Jesus, when he had found a young ass, sat thereon; as it is written,[15] Fear not, daughter of Sion: behold, thy King cometh, sitting on an ass's colt.[16] These things understood not his disciples at the first: but when Jesus was glorified, then remembered they that these things were written of him, and that they had done these things unto him.[17] The people therefore that was with him when he called Lazarus out of his grave, and raised him from the dead, bare record.[18] For this cause the people also met him, for that they heard that he had done this miracle.[19] The Pharisees therefore said among themselves, Perceive ye how ye prevail nothing? behold, the world is gone after him.[20] And there were certain Greeks among them that came up to worship at the feast:[21] The same came therefore to Philip, which was of Bethsaida of Galilee, and desired him, saying, Sir, we would see Jesus.[22] Philip cometh and telleth Andrew: and again Andrew and Philip tell Jesus[23] And Jesus answered them, saying, The hour is come, that the Son of man should be glorified.[24] Verily, verily, I say unto you, Except a corn of wheat fall into the ground and die, it abideth alone: but if it die, it bringeth forth much fruit.[25] He that loveth his life shall lose it; and he that hateth his life in this world shall keep it unto life eternal.[26] If any man serve me, let him follow me; and where I am, there shall also my servant be: if any man serve me, him will my Father honour.[27] Now is my soul troubled; and what shall I say? Father, save me from this hour: but for this cause came I unto this hour.[28] Father, glorify thy name. Then came there a voice from heaven, saying, I have both glorified it, and will glorify it again.[29] The people therefore, that stood by, and heard it, said that it thundered: others said, An angel spake to him.[30] Jesus answered and said, This voice came not because of me, but for your sakes.[31] Now is the judgment of this world: now shall the prince of this world be cast out.[32] And I, if I be lifted up from the earth, will draw all men unto me.[33] This he said, signifying what death he should die.[34] The people answered him, We have heard out of the law that Christ abideth for ever: and how sayest thou, The Son of man must be lifted up? who is this Son of man?[35] Then Jesus said unto them, Yet a little while is the light with you. Walk while ye have the light, lest darkness come upon you: for he that walketh in darkness knoweth not whither he goeth.[36] While ye have light, believe in the light, that ye may be the children of light. These things spake Jesus, and departed, and did hide himself from them.[37] But though he had done so many miracles before them, yet they believed not on him:[38] That the saying of Esaias the prophet might be fulfilled, which he spake, Lord, who hath believed our report? and to whom hath the arm of the Lord been revealed?[39] Therefore they could not believe, because that Esaias said again,[40] He hath blinded their eyes, and hardened their heart; that they should not see with their eyes, nor understand with their heart, and be converted, and I should heal them.[41] These things said Esaias, when he saw his glory, and spake of him.[42] Nevertheless among the chief rulers also many believed on him; but because of the Pharisees they did not confess him, lest they should be put out of the synagogue:[43] For they loved the praise of men more than the praise of God.[44] Jesus cried and said, He that believeth on me, believeth not on me, but on him that sent me.[45] And he that seeth me seeth him that sent me.[46] I am come a light into the world, that whosoever believeth on me should not abide in darkness.[47] And if any man hear my words, and believe not, I judge him not: for I came not to judge the world, but to save the world.[48] He that rejecteth me, and receiveth not my words, hath one that judgeth him: the word that I have spoken, the same shall judge him in the last day

.[49] For I have not spoken of myself; but the Father which sent me, he gave me a commandment, what I should say, and what I should speak.[50] And I know that his commandment is life everlasting: whatsoever I speak therefore...

even as the Father said unto me, so I speak.

THIS IS NOT THE END IT IS JUST THE BEGINNING

Appendix

All scripture is from the King James Bible taken from www.Biblegateway.com

All quotations are personal conversations between Jeff & subject, except on page 43 Thomas Jefferson; www.Monticello.org

On page 24 & 25 There is a reference to a lesson from Zig Ziglar. These are personal notes from a BBQ w/Zig at Marine Air Force Base MIRAMAR, San Diego, CA March 2004

All other views expressed and written are the collective thoughts of life personal experiences... it is still free to think... this can be construed as free thought, free thinking , and of universal domain.

All photos taken by God in Motion Ministries, Taylor, MI 48180 available on Facebook/Godinmotionministry Larry

Photos in order of appearance

1. Front Cover: Trenton Michigan (hidden scripture photo retouch)
2. Page 5 Trenton Michigan
3. Page 8 Family Fun Flat Rock Michigan
4. Page 9 Trenton Michigan
5. Page 21 Trenton Michigan
6. Page 28 Jeff & Selah Jones
7. Page 35 Lincoln Park Michigan
8. Page 44 Taylor Michigan
9. Page 50 Lincoln Park Michigan
10. Page 71 Melvindale Michigan
11. Page 79 Taylor Michigan
12. Page 86 Jeff Jones
13. Page 88 Living Life Full Random
14. Rear Cover Trenton Michigan

Jeff is married to his lovely wife Brenda. He has 11 children and 8 grandchildren. He has over 20 years of successful history in sales and sales management. He has been in ministry for over 20 years, as well. He is a licensed professional of financial services and entrepreneur of several enterprises. He loves people. He loves the interaction and the exchange of ideas and words. His poetry has been published multiple times and is named amongst the greatest poets of the decade. He is currently completing a life project series of children's stories with his own illustrations, a unique business series, an historical fiction, and a marriage workbook. He is currently running for United States Senate in Michigan. He is a visionary and idea man.

Learning to love like GOD!

Now Pause!

Made in the USA
San Bernardino, CA
13 March 2014